Thriving Throughout Your Retirement Transition

Retirement Coaches Association

Table of Contents

Introduction

What if you could assemble an all-star team of superheroes with a diverse collection of superpowers? I'm talking about people with advanced degrees, c-suite experience, practical knowledge from decades in the trenches, and a laundry list of accolades, awards, and testimonials to back it all up.

What would you do with them and how would you harness both their power and desire to do good in the world?

It's the situation I was faced with four years ago when I created the Retirement Coaches Association – and the challenge I face each year when we take on a new writing project like this.

The good news about organizing a group of all-star superheroes is that they always come through. They show up and deliver, and that's exactly what you get with *Thriving Throughout Your Retirement Transition*.

It's an action-packed collection of wisdom, insights, fresh perspective, and concrete action steps. All essential elements to one of the most highly sought-after phases of life but also one of the most misunderstood.

Retirement today is not only different than ever before, but the impact from a global pandemic has kicked open the door to a whole new set of challenges and opportunities.

The Coronavirus may end up being one of the greatest turning points in the history of retirement planning.

It's an unprecedented time and situation because the cause of the stock market meltdown and subsequent shift in the way we work and live is not just financial. It's personal in terms of health and well-being, and it's affecting people mentally, physically, socially, and spiritually.

It has ushered in a new narrative around the concept of Retirement Wellness, where your mental, social, physical, and spiritual well-being are equally as important as your financial health and well-being.

Now more than ever, people need new, fresh perspectives, concrete ideas, actionable strategies, and leaders to help them thrive in both the time leading up to retirement and well into it.

Our commitment to you is that you will find those factors and much more in the pages that follow. We have assembled a dynamic collection of retirement planning advice and wisdom that goes beyond the more traditional measures of money, and squarely puts the focus on you as the individual or couple. Just as it should be!

We hope you enjoy our life's work and desire to make an impact on both you and the retirement planning industry. Don't feel confined to following the normal page rules or reading this book in sequential order. Stroll through the material at your own pace, taking time to stop and enjoy this new and life-changing perspective on life in retirement.

Please feel free to learn more about our organization or share your thoughts and feedback with us at www.RetirementCoachesAssociation.org. Additionally, take the time to connect with individual authors based on their contact information available at the end of each chapter.

Here's to changing the world of retirement, one reader, chapter, and coach at a time.

Sincerely,

Robert Laura

Founder, Retirement Coaches Association

Retirementhood™: Next Exit
By Sue Mintz

First things first. It's not unusual that I am asked to explain Retirementhood: Next Exit, so let's unpack what it means.

You travel through different phases during your lifetime – childhood, adulthood, parenthood, and so on – all of which bring natural changes. Just as moving into a new residence brings you into a new neighborhood, transitioning from a career into retirement takes you into Retirementhood.

The transition is not as simple as leaving your last day of work and then, *poof*, Retirementhood. For your time in Retirementhood to be successful and fulfilling, a balanced exit plan is critical. It's only safe to take the exit once you have established both a financial and nonfinancial plan, and it's best to begin preparing miles before you decide to take the exit.

"What and how have you been planning for retirement?" is a question I ask potential clients when visiting with them for the first time. This helps me learn where they are in the planning process. The majority of the time, the answer is they have been contributing to a retirement savings account and meeting with a financial advisor.

I applaud them for saving money and preparing for long-term financial security, but they come to me (a nonfinancial retirement coach), because there is another huge component to retirement that is completely separate from financial security. Preparing for the nonfinancial side of retirement includes taking into account what brings fulfillment, purpose, joy, good health, fun times and what allows you to become who you want to be.

So how do we create a plan that does all these things?

Throughout your work and life experiences, you become aware of what you depend on to satisfy, motivate, and drive yourself. You know what gives you a reason to get out of bed every morning (other than a good cup of coffee). When you enter Retirementhood, you still need a motivator, whether it be a hobby or an experience, that's going to give you a reason to start your day.

Many soon-to-be retirees have a pretty good idea of how they will fill their days with intentional and purposeful activities. Other retirees haven't realized its importance, thinking mainly about getting out of the daily grind of work and replacing their first conference call with a morning TV show. Then it's off to the gym or the golf course, an errand, then lunch, and a nap. Don't get me wrong; this kind of day is well deserved and perfectly okay once in a while, but days with structure and purpose will lead to a healthier and more fulfilling retirement.

Let's think about what motivated you in any of your jobs. Was it feeling valued? Was it having structure in your day and having something to which you could look forward to? How important was your social network? What about continuing to learn and keeping up with what's going on in the world around you? Making a difference in people's lives or a company's brand? Feeling empowered or given the opportunity to demonstrate creativity? What else?

And what happens to those motivators when you retire? They dissolve and collapse.

This is why, before entering Retirementhood, it's important to understand how to replace or maintain what satisfies and motivates you. You can also find something completely new that will give you the same joy and level of fulfillment.

For example, Alice is preparing for retirement. She is comfortable with her financial plan and is confident it will serve her well. In addition to her role as a commercial real estate broker, she has been mentoring women in her network by sharing the expertise, skills, and resources that have contributed to her success. So, after closing her office door for the last time, she not only has a plan to spend time with her husband and family, participate in leisure activities she enjoys, and focus on her health; she can also continue to mentor young women new to her industry and apply these skills elsewhere in her community.

Since age 14, Kathy was fascinated by medicine and caring for the elderly because she spent so much time with her grandparents. After her career as an attorney and then a stay-at-home mom, at age 52 she and her husband became empty nesters. They sat down with their financial advisor and felt comfortable with their financial plan, which allowed for Kathy to go to nursing school. Her nonfinancial plan included going back to school and receiving her nursing degree, bringing her the fulfillment of working in nursing home facilities she had wanted since she was a teenager.

Once you have prepared your plan for what will contribute to a healthy, purposeful, and fun retirement, and you are feeling financially and emotionally ready, it's time to put your blinker on and move into the lane for the exit into Retirementhood. Without a balanced plan that includes both financial and motivational aspects, you might have many unfulfilling years, potentially leading to mental, emotional, and physical health issues. It's not unusual to "flunk" retirement because your plan wasn't balanced. In Michael Stein's book, *The Prosperous Retirement: Guide to the New Reality*, he wrote "Most retirements will fail because of nonfinancial reasons rather than financial ones." With money in the bank you may sleep well at night, but you won't have a reason to get out of bed in the morning.

Jack had the textbook career success story. He started out in sales and climbed the corporate ladder. After a 30-year career, he retired from the third company he worked for as their vice president of global sales. He was diligent about meeting with his financial advisor every quarter. They put together a financial plan that was sure to cover living expenses, adventures, and an inheritance for his children.

Along came retirement. His colleagues threw him an all-out going away party, and three days later, he took his family on a cruise. It wasn't long before he was back at home binge watching Netflix, playing solitaire, playing golf a few times a week, and maybe running an errand or two. More than anything, he was waiting for his wife to come home from work. His daily routine was vastly different than what he was used to, and he became depressed. He no longer felt like he was making a difference, he missed socializing, and his health suffered. He had not thought about how he would replace the structure of his work routine with a fulfilling new lifestyle. By creating a plan before exiting into Retirementhood, Jack could have saved himself the physical and emotional stress of his transition.

Before moving into Retirementhood, you need to know what you will be packing up and leaving behind. Think about your work, your daily structure, your purpose, your passion, your title, your teammates, your stress, your management team, your responsibilities, your customers, and continuous learning opportunities. There's no doubt you'll be happy to leave some things behind, but there will also be parts that you will miss. Which of those were most important and fulfilling? Does your plan include ways for you to replace these things?

When you miss some or all of what you're leaving behind, just remember you can replace those losses with gains. What will be your new daily structure? What will be your purpose? How can you create a new social network? Might you want to use your knowledge and skills in a new environment? Are you thinking about giving back to causes you are passionate about? Is there something in your community that would benefit from you and your past experiences?

Entering a new phase in life offers new opportunities to grow, mature, enhance, and enjoy new experiences. Each phase also brings its challenges and uncertainties. Exiting from your career and entering Retirementhood is no different. It is much more than being the center of attention at a retirement party or taking a retirement cruise. It's not an event; it's a process.

Similar to a GPS used to help navigate traveling in your car, an RPS (Retirement Planning System) helps navigate your journey through Retirementhood.

Upon exiting into Retirementhood, you will see on your RPS that you may travel through three to four different communities: Honeymoon Beach, Pity City Park, and Now What? Crossing, before arriving at The New Normal Estates.

Your first stop may be Honeymoon Beach, an exciting community you have planned for and can't wait to visit. You may even get a speeding ticket when you see this destination in front of you and your career in your rear-view mirror. This might manifest as a vacation to a country you've been daydreaming about for years. Maybe it's a spa or a place where all you do is lay on the beach and relax drinking piña coladas. It could be waking up at home and just doing what you want to do when you want to do it. Wherever your Honeymoon Beach is, it's a well-deserved reward you gave yourself when you retired. How long you stay there will depend on how you are feeling, and how soon you want to set your RPS for directions to move on to Now What? Crossing.

Pity City Park may also be the first community you visit. "Visit" is the key word here; you don't want to stay long. Rather than Honeymoon Beach, this could be your first stop, because, for one reason or another, you are not happy about retiring. Perhaps retirement was involuntary because of a company decision to downsize, a family situation that brought you back home, or because of your own declining health. Depending on your attitude, how you respond to this unexpected scenario, and how you adapt to the change, you may speed through, proceed with caution, or get stuck and need help moving on to Now What? Crossing. When you are in Pity City Park, make sure you keep your RPS active, and emergency numbers handy. You may need to contact a retirement coach to help tow you out if you get stuck and need help to get moving again and on to Now What? Crossing.

The next community, Now What? Crossing is where you solidify the nonfinancial plans you made prior to retiring, or create your plan if you didn't do this before retiring. What's going to motivate you? How are you going to replace the ways you felt satisfied and purposeful before you retired? What's going to get you out of bed in the morning other than a good cup of coffee? What else do you believe is important to include in your plan? And of course, what are you happy to leave behind? For now, you may want to turn your RPS off for a while to take time to prepare or review your plan. Do you want to keep the plan "as is" or make some changes? Do you want to experiment with some of the plans you made? Maybe you're just not sure, and want a sanity check with your retirement coach before moving into New Normal Estates. Don't be afraid to reach out to him/her. That's what a coach is for – to help map out the paths you want to follow after you enter New Normal Estates.

Before entering the New Normal Estates, make sure your RPS is back on and follow the different paths you set for yourself. Do these paths take you to places that bring you fulfillment in your new normal lifestyle? Do you belong to one of the groups below, which Gail M. McDonald and Marilyn Bushey identify in their book, *Retirement Your Way*, or do you create one all for yourself?

- **The Traditionalist** stops working and engages in a variety of non-paid, mostly leisure activities.

- **The Altruist** stops working and instead volunteers, as a board member or in other roles.
- **The Lifelong Learner** stops working and pursues a non-paid activity that requires significant practice or continued learning.
- **The Stair Stepper** continues to work in the same career, while gradually cutting back.
- **The Boomeranger** takes a break and then returns to work.
- **The Reinventor** continues to work in a career or another role.

But wait, what if something isn't working out the way you wanted? That's normal and it's okay. Is your RPS on? Do you want to make a U-turn, go back to Now What? Crossing and make some adjustments in your plan? Don't be afraid to reach out to your coach, revise your plan, and then come back to New Normal Estates. Remember Jack? Before retirement he didn't put together a plan that would bring him purpose, fulfillment, and good health, so he made a U-turn and set up an appointment with a retirement transition coach. Through their time together, they created a plan for him to volunteer in the community and use the skills that made him successful while working. Serving as a volunteer for a cause he was passionate about, and using skills he missed using since working, brought him back to feeling a sense of purpose and that he was making a difference. And as a bonus, through volunteering, he connected with a new group of like-minded folks he became friends with. The plan also included time with a personal trainer twice a week, as well as a round or two of golf!

As you travel through these different communities, it's not unusual to run into roadblocks, stop at rest areas, and you may even hit a curb. And that's okay as long as you respond with a positive attitude and know there will always be family, friends, your coach, and your RPS to bring you back to the road and enjoy your time in Retirementhood.

Remember that retirement is always about positivity and moving forward. *You're not retiring from a career,* you're *entering Retirementhood.* Best of luck settling in!

About The Author

Sue Mintz's background includes over 25 years at a Fortune 500 company, where she excelled in management and leadership development training, career coaching, and corporate communications. Sue is a certified retirement transition coach, career coach, workshop facilitator, speaker, and writer. As a retirement transition coach, she helps clients plan for the non-financial side of retirement by taking them from their career to "something else", where they will feel purposeful, healthy, and energized in this new phase of their life. She received her retirement coaching certification through Retirement Options, a division of Career Partners International LLC and is a member of the Retirement Coaches Association.

Sue is also a certified "Now What?"® coach/facilitator. The "Now What?" program is a proven process that helps clients wanting to make a change in their career find clarity on what will bring fulfillment, meaning and joy in the next phase of their employment.

Learn more about Sue, founder of Retirementhood™, at www.Retirementhood.com.

References

Gail M. McDonald and Marilyn Bushey, *Retirement Your Way*, Dallas, TX: Choices Next, 2019.

Michael Stein, *The Prosperous Retirement: Guide to the New Reality*, EMSTCO, 1998.

What No One Tells You About
The Roller Coaster Of Retirement
By Kaendi Munguti

If you are like me, you most probably have been cruising through life without giving much thought to the prospect of retirement. Now, you probably have a pension plan and some savings. You are highly qualified and well respected in your area of work; you do not feel that old after all, and retirement is the last thing on your mind. However, everyone in your workplace is younger than you, and there is a mandatory retirement age. You start to experience the dissonance between your chronological and biological age. Over time, the reality becomes clear – you begin to ask yourself the "what next" question.

Over the last several years, I have been very aware of my impending retirement. There have been many times I wished for a scripted and structured guide of "how to" to prepare for retirement. Unfortunately, this is not the case. One of the things that no one tells you about retirement is how to transition from your life in the workplace (after more than thirty years in my case) into retirement. Although there are indeed numerous resources to help you make this transition, the information can be overwhelming, daunting, and downright confusing. I have spent an excessive amount of time trying to figure all this out. One of the things that I did during this time was to delve more into understanding the issues facing imminent retirees like myself and in the process even trained to be a retirement coach. This knowledge has helped me to have a better appreciation of the challenges many of us face in trying to figure out what to do once we leave the workplace (*aka* retirement).

Undoubtedly, each person's transition to retirement is unique. Nevertheless, from my discussions and conversations with colleagues and friends who have retired, some commonalities emerge. These include the uncertainty, fear of the unknown and, concerns that the decision of what to do in retirement will be the correct one. Trying to visualize your future in retirement, knowing that there are no guarantees and limited time for "do-overs," can be unsettling. It is undeniable that we all respond to the changes occasioned by retirement differently. For example, for those of us who like structure in our lives, the same may permeate how we approach retirement. For others, it may involve retiring and then trying to figure out what to do once they have retired. What I have learned in this process is that it is essential to start preparing or at least have a tentative plan (if possible) that articulates what you are retiring to. There is evidence to show that planning is vital in defining retirement outcomes.

Although we still use the term retirement, it is recognized that its use in today's world may not be appropriate. Traditional perceptions and stereotypes attached to the idea of retirement persist. There is no doubt the word is a misnomer, and a new concept is required to define the transition that reflects the engaged and active lifestyles of today's retirees. Views of retirement may, in part, explain why it is sometimes difficult for many of us to come to terms with the end of work life and transition to the next phase of our lives.

As a Kenyan, discussions of retirement with family and friends is compounded by their concerns about "how well I will fare" once I retire. The outcome of this is always the ever-nagging feeling and doubt on my part that my plans will work as I have laid them out. While social support from one's family and friends is essential as one transitions to retirement for many of us, these social networks are unprepared to provide the cushion and assistance we may need as we move towards retirement.

In general, my impending retirement has not been perceived as a possibility for better opportunities; rather a cause for worry about my life in retirement. These concerns are in part because, for a long time, retirement in Kenya has been synonymous with death. Many stories are told of the retiree who, upon retirement, went to their village, woke up every morning and read the newspaper, had no social relations with people in his community, was lonely and did not live or enjoy their retirement for long. While this may be true in some cases, what has been missing in this narrative is the fact that there has been a lack of trained retirement coaches to support prospective retirees in preparing actionable plans focusing on the nonfinancial and financial aspects of their lives in retirement. There has been limited discussion on retirement planning, and this needs to change. It is important that we redefine the meaning of retirement and ensure that those who are retiring have the information, skills, and ability to plan, live, enjoy, and thrive during the second and third phases of their lives (their *Tena* life).

While the pessimism about retirement may be based on people's experiences – where people have had difficulties in retirement due to either illness, financial challenges, or other factors – this is not unique to retirees. There needs to be dialogue in the retirement sphere of how one's friends and family can be supportive in easing the transition.

A recent study looking at the discourses of retirement in the United States in the print media discusses how information may shape perceptions on retirement. One of the key findings was that much of the discourses on retirement overwhelmingly focus on being financially prepared with pessimistic views on retiree's preparedness. Besides, these discussions tend to be contradictory.[1] It is no wonder that many of us face the prospect of retirement with uncertainty and trepidation.

Unlike the better-defined career trajectory – getting an education, training, and qualifications for a defined job and entering the workplace – there is no clear road map on how to prepare for retirement.

Through the various phases of this journey, the elusive questions for me have always been: What will retirement life look like? What will I do? How will

I stay engaged and continue to live the middle-class lifestyle I am used to? Should I retire completely from my workplace? Work part-time? Start a new career? How can I use my knowledge and skills to impact society in a different capacity? It has been a process of endless possibilities – but no defined pathway on how to turn my dreams and aspirations into reality. This is exacerbated by the knowledge that without proper planning and preparation for the transition to retirement, one can also experience what has been termed the "dark side of retirement," characterized by, among other things, loss of financial resources due to poor investments, depression, and substance abuse, etc.

What no one tells you about retirement is that the prospect of an impending retirement can be daunting and is a roller coaster ride. Not because you are afraid of leaving the workplace (although this may be the case for some) or acknowledging that we are of a "certain age," but simply because many of us do not know what to do next. We are afraid of the unknown. More so for those of us who know too well that life in retirement is unlikely to be "one long vacation." No one ever tells you that trying to figure out your life in retirement has many ups and downs. The process is tempered with the excitement of a life where you define the future in your terms but also tremendous concerns about your ability to ensure you live a happy and comfortable life in retirement.

After my initial foreboding and indecision, I decided to take a more proactive role in my transition to retirement. I started from where I know best – reading everything I could get with information on retirement, including the experiences of others who had retired. I then began to have a better understanding of the various nuances of retirement and the uniqueness of this to each one of us.

While not everyone may want to read a mundane subject like retirement, I believe that we are all well placed and have access to various sources of information (however contradictory they may be), including social media. It is crucial to determine the value (if any) of information shaping your retirement decisions. Through this process, one of the most surprising aspects was the realization that what I was experiencing was common among prospective retirees. I also realized that there are qualified and caring retirement coaches who can walk with you through this journey with a holistic focus on planning a "no-regrets retirement" beyond the financial aspects.

What else have I learned? I have come to learn that there are things that you can do – but most important is to take control of your destiny and start a process of planning (not necessary in a formal manner) but identifying and answering the "what next" question. Below are some suggestions based on my experiences and in discussion with others.

Validate Your Feelings

While not everyone who is facing an impending retirement has uncertainties and fears about the future, talking to people in a similar situation has validated my feelings. It is essential to know that you are not alone and that any apprehensions you may have – whether concerns about your financial security, or remaining relevant, healthy, and engaged – are valid. This consciousness and awareness are vital in ensuring that your feelings do not paralyze you to inaction.

Turn Your Fears Into Focus

One of my favorite books is *Feel the Fear and Do It Anyway* by Susan Jaffers.[2] A key takeaway for me from this book is, whatever your fear – whether it is aging, an ending of a career or, a new beginning – fear is a fact of life rather than a barrier to success. In her book, she defines level one fears as those that happen (like aging and retirement) and level two as those fears that require actions. In my view, though we have fears of things that will occur in the course of our lifetime, these fears also need action, such as ensuring healthy aging and active and purposeful retirement. We tend to be afraid of retirement because of the uncertainties of the future. As noted earlier, you most likely have more questions than answers on how your life in retirement will be. At this point, many of us are merely searching for purpose and meaning of life in retirement.

Your anxieties and fears are further compounded by the numerous and confusing information on retirement. Based on experience, it is imperative to acknowledge your worries as you identify and define the way forward in retirement. It is necessary to be practical in determining the next chapter of your life. You may have to try out different ideas as you plan. You have to believe that as one dream is ending, another will become a reality.

No Need To 'Teach An Old Dog New Tricks'

By the time to reach the age where you are planning to retire from the workplace – you most likely have all the "tricks" you need to prepare for the retirement you deserve - although it may not seem that way. This is in part because of has been called "crystallized intelligence,"[3] which is our ability to use learned knowledge and experience. One way to do this is to identify your skills, expertise, and experiences and determine how you may want to use these as you delineate your life in retirement. You already have the power to impart influence on your retirement. As the Swahili saying goes, *kuishi kwingi ni kuona mengi* – experience comes with age!

As a social scientist and teacher, when thinking of my retirement, I started by taking an internal inventory of the skills and experiences that I can bring to bear in my "second" life. It quickly became clear to me that while I may be able to do some part-time teaching at a university, I would not be seeking full-time employment, nor would I be starting a business for which I had no prior training or experience. I started by taking online courses and getting certification in motivational speaking and retirement coaching. While I did become certified in these areas, I was still not sure how I would use my newly acquired skills. My struggles with an imminent retirement led me to read more and educate myself on the issues around retirement. I have since started my own retirement business and look forward to using the lessons learned in this process to work with others who may find themselves in the roller coaster of retirement. I hope to learn from them and to address together the issues facing our generation and making the transition to retirement less frightening and a reality to be embraced and not dreaded.

Start Writing Your Own 'Job' Description

It is vital to create a mental image of your future and work toward it. Just like we prepare for careers and work-life, there is no reason why we should not use the same approach to plan for life in retirement. A friend recently compared the transition to retirement with adolescence – a time when many of us feel unmoored, drifting, knowing that a critical change is happening in your life, but with less clarity on what you need to do or how to do it. Some tend to make this transition with less thoughtfulness, and go into this uncharted territory with little or no preparation.

Planning for retirement is critical to one's success. One of the most significant examples for me is my mother. She passed away five years ago, more than twenty years after retiring. She was a planner and, before retirement, started her own small retail business. After several years, she bought her premises (to stop paying rent) and continued to grow her business. She lived life on her terms – active, engaged in giving back to the community, having an independent income, and creating a vast social network and friendships over the years. I continue to use her as a role model as I write my new "job" description (no pun intended) for my retirement.

Have A Plan For Your Life In Retirement

While pre-retirement planning is critical in defining retirement outcomes, many workplaces do not offer support for their staff in preparing for retirement. There may be in-house training, workshops, and seminars on retirement – but many of these tend to be a one-off with no follow-up support. Also, many of them tend to focus on financial planning with little or no attention to the nonfinancial issues of retirement, such as physical, mental, and social life.

Undeniably, well-thought-out, and planned retirement can lead to new opportunities. However, it is common to see people retire without any forethought or plan on what they will do once they leave the workplace. Recently, a colleague was retiring after many years of working in the same institution. During one of those infamous retirement parties, he was asked what he planned to do in retirement. He explained that he intended to start a farming business and grow exotic mangoes. After further discussion, it was clear that he had not given much thought to this business idea, including its viability, for example, how long it would take for the mangoes to grow and be available for sale, the market for this kind of product, labor costs, etc. The moral of the story is that while this may be a good idea, it is imperative to have a good understanding of your plans in retirement as part of a well-thought-out pre-retirement plan. Whereas there are no guarantees and retirement planning has many uncertainties (and plans will most likely keep evolving), you can avoid some of the significant downfalls among newly retired people – such as investing time and resources into projects that are not well thought out and more likely to fail due to lack of proper conceptualization and planning.

Enjoy The Ride Into Your Retirement Life

The term "roller coaster" has more than one meaning, and it can be a source of great enjoyment and excitement in amusement parks. Hopefully, for Baby Boomers and future generations, planning for retirement will be less of a maze and more of an exciting prospect after many years spent in the workplace. My journey has allowed me to dig deeper and understand the "world" of retirement. As a trained retirement coach, I look forward to the opportunity to impact the lives of others who are planning the transition to retirement and defining the second half of their lives. I firmly believe we each can ensure that despite the ups and downs of retirement – you enjoy the ride. Whatever plans you have for the second and third phase of your life – it should include all aspects of retirement planning beyond the financial issues.

Just as in life, everything is unlikely to go smoothly in retirement. Most important is to have coping strategies to navigate the tough times and the flexibility and adaptability to face any challenges that may arise and thrive in retirement. I am not there yet, but I can say with certainty that I have less fear and more conviction about my life in retirement, and for now – despite the crisis facing the world with COVID-19 – I feel more confident about the future than ever before.

About The Author

Kaendi Munguti has a Ph.D. and a master's degree in Public Health (MPH) from the University of California, Los Angeles, and a BA and MA in Sociology. Over the last twenty years, she has worked in international development with an emphasis on public health. She has worked with, among others, the World Health Organization and Jhpiego (An affiliate of Johns Hopkins University). She has also worked with Kalamazoo College as a study-abroad director for their exchange program in Kenya. She is widely traveled and has worked and lived in different countries. She is a trained retirement coach and a member of the Retirement Coaches Association (RCA). She can be reached at kaendimunguti@entenalife.com.

References

1. Patricia E. Gettings, "Discourses of Retirement in the United States," *Work, Aging and Retirement,* 4 (4), 315-329.

2. Susan Jaffers, *Feel the Fear and Do it Anyway,* London: Reed Elsevier, 2014.

3. Cattell, R. B. "Theory of Fluid and Crystallized intelligence: A Critical Experiment. *Journal of Educational Psychology, 54*(1), 1963, 1–22.

The Art Of Perspective, Vision, And Choice: Transitioning With Excitement Vs. Anxiety
By Barbara Archer

Thump, thump, thump, thump…should my heart be beating this fast? And in my ears as well? Am I having shortness of breath? What is this feeling in my stomach?

Is this a heart attack? Anxiety? Fear? Or simply *excitement*? Oh my, that's it – change is in the air and I'm going to retire!

Any time we make a significant life transition there can be enormous physical cues and emotions that go along with it. Looking back at past experiences when your life shifted, were your feelings of anticipation positive or negative? Were you excited or worried? Did you rush in or hang back? Do you even remember?

I have vivid memories of my first job in the mid-1970s as a new college graduate. I was working as the only woman supervisor on the third shift in an automotive manufacturing plant without a women's restroom. No discrimination was intended – no women meant no need for a separate restroom! I recall the heat of machinery, the smell of oil, the yellowish lights, and that overriding sound of the *thump, thump, thump* of *my* heart. *How,* I nervously wondered, *could I direct men two to three times my age to improve their skills and teach them new techniques to increase the quality of our lab testing facility?* Looking back in my rearview mirror and adding perspective, it was a wonderful, challenging experience where we all learned together and built a fun cooperative team.

This initial adventure gave me the confidence to later start a business in another male-dominated field – that of wealth management. I have helped plan retirement for friends and clients while managing hundreds of millions of dollars. With decades of knowledge accumulated from their colorful stories, honest conversations, and shared experiences, I readily accepted that there was more to crafting a successful retirement than measuring monetary wealth. It is with this awareness I now help guide others through this passage to a new lifestyle.

Now join me in reminiscing on *your* first day of school, graduating from college, starting a new job, getting married, or having a child. How did it feel? Was it as good or as bad as you anticipated? Either way, you survived it and perhaps have a different perspective looking back on those past events. Time and distance color our memories and we have the power to choose the color.

The English language has provided us with emotional colors, including "I feel blue," "He was green with envy," and "She was seeing red." My personal favorite coined by my husband, is "I'm orange today." He has identified orange as a lonely color – not quite sunny yellow or passionate red, but alone and in between, despite color psychology saying orange is playful and energetic. Once again, it's the beauty of choice. As you think about retirement, what shade do you envision and why? Have you prepared your palette to paint your future? Perhaps your three favorite colors are green, blue, and white as a perfect layup for golf or ideal for a beach walk. Maybe yours is yellow, pink, and purple, thinking of cocktails at sunset. As the artist of your yet unnamed masterpiece of retirement, the blank canvas is yours to own and create, so let's do so with enthusiasm!

Perspective

As we age, memories play an important part in our mental health where positive memories can generate positive emotions. As a parent, I can remember tears from a child having "the worst day ever." And trying to have her identify and verbalize her feelings as being sad, embarrassed, frustrated, lonely, hurt, frightened, or insecure. Other than hugs for comfort and reassurance of a happier future, I knew I had to offer a way to help this young child find a way to self-soothe, as there would be similar days ahead at school, at work, or in a relationship. My question was a simple one. What happened a year ago today that might have made you feel this same way? Invariably the answer was, "I don't remember." And that is the point. This too shall pass. In recognizing how we are feeling now and knowing that next year at this time we might not even remember the angst, it can be enormously reassuring. Our perspective or point of view changes as time passes. With longer time from the event, we accumulate more knowledge and experience and can identify what is truly important to us. And that distance has the ability to make the good memories so much sweeter and sometimes the awkward ones become humorous stories.

It is our turn to confront a new surge of colorful emotions, and with increased wisdom and experience we can make shifts in our new lifestyles. Let's address this age-old practice of accepting change and consider how we might do so with more grace and elegance.

Let's start by learning some "perspective" tricks to help you enjoy your new phase in life. We will use the art of perspective to our advantage, along with vision, to imagine a scenario and then make choices.

Perspective and Control: What can you control? Picture your last social engagement. Was the evening spent with friends energizing or deflating? You can select how you spend time and with whom, so choose wisely. Do you devour the news or stock reports first thing in the morning or before bed – how will you use that information and how does that influence your day or your ability to sleep?

Perspective and Response: Try reframing your future story to feel excitement over anxiety. If this is new to you, be patient as this takes confidence and practice. Once you begin to get that "feeling," take three deep breaths then identify and name the emotion. Next, choose your response with positive self-talk – from rough waters to surf's up. You didn't get the dream house contract, but there might be a better one yet. Dreading a long plane ride resurfaced to focus on the reward at the end – a new country, seeing family, or closing a deal. Take an anxiety-inducing thought and play a game with it – turn it around to a positive, fun, and exciting thought.

Perspective and Preparation: Prepare and plan while envisioning that all will be well. With planning, bumps in the road can be just that – bumps. Part of the plan can be expecting the unexpected and treating the bump as an opportunity. Opportunities such as:

- Delayed flight? Time to get that new book at the airport bookstore.
- Concert performance canceled? Opportunity for a game night at home.
- The ballgame is rained out? The chance to try a new restaurant since you are downtown anyway.

Perspective and Memory: Significant days like a wedding, the birth of a child, a graduation, or a first job have a better tendency to stick and they are filled with emotions and memories. Reflect on your important events. What do you see? Smell? Feel? Taste? Hear? Is there someone that was there with you to share the memories? Have you done so recently? It may be time to conjure up some special past moments and share with those close to you.

Perspective Exercise: On this day, a year ago, what good happened? What was not so good? Do you even remember (without looking at your journal or calendar)? A year from now, will you remember this day? How will you describe it to yourself? What is important about this moment now? Will it hold the same importance in a year? Five years? Ten years or more?

Vision

As we contemplate our transition to a new lifestyle, let's envision ideal yet realistic mental pictures. For some it might be a more bucolic environment with a life enveloped in quiet times with close family members and jaunts for picnics and fishing. For others, it might present bustling opportunities to cheer on their sports team or be swept away at a cultural event followed by sharing dinner with friends to relive the experience. Do you conjure up the glamour and intrigue of exotic or adventure travel, or wish to pursue serving a worthy and charitable mission to make an impact in a community? Or perhaps you want to do it all and you view this next chapter as an unlimited choice of colors.

This empty canvas can be delightfully challenging or overwhelmingly confusing, and here is where can begin: in our word selection. Why not be delightfully confused and enjoy the process, as in beginning a puzzle or drawing an outline of your vision. By the way, in using the term overwhelmingly, it occurred to me I couldn't recall the word "whelm" used in any of my recently read literature, and curiosity got the best of me. When used as a verb, whelm can sound frightening as it engulfs, submerges, or buries. But when used as a noun, it is the act of flowing or heaping up abundantly, and thus can feel reassuring; I look forward to using this word in this way.

Are you as curious today as when you were a child? Here is a wonderful way for us to stay mentally fit and psychically young to keep the positive emotions flowing – learn a new language, instrument, card game, sport, or skill, or investigate new cultures, religions, books, neighborhoods, restaurants, or simply meet new people and be interested in learning more about them. With Google, YouTube, and the ever-present online library, we have no excuse for not pursuing new passions. By trying something new we are challenging ourselves to be energized and to have fun while pursuing it alone or with a partner.

Choice

We all want a successful retirement. Stanford University psychologist Carol Dweck has researched that attitudes can color our success, identifying differences between a fixed and growth mindset. A fixed mindset tilts toward negative certainty while a growth mindset will take the opposite view. A growth mindset views challenges as opportunities, not obstacles, feedback as constructive and not criticism, and helping others as inspirational and not a chore. Yet again, with a growth mindset we can take a negative word like "chore" and find it to be uplifting. I had an uncle that found daily chores as a form of meditation – from cutting beans, to folding laundry, to mopping a floor. With little mental capacity required to execute most mundane daily housework, it allows the mind to choose to wander or focus. Depending on your spiritual intent, it provides a lovely time to either rest the brain or solve the latest conundrum while accomplishing the task at hand and engaging a growth mindset.

In pursuit of a successful next chapter in our lives, let's focus on this growth mindset. What self-talk will help you move forward with fun? Will you be the kernel or the popcorn? The dense fog or the floating mist? Will the quiet times feel desolate or peaceful? Will you quit a new pursuit or just pause? Did you feel a squeeze or a hug? Is that item drifting or flowing? And to think you have all that control to interpret such moments which make up your day.

Now that we have explored how perspective, vision, and choice color our world, let's venture into your own personal plan for retirement. The key components we want to contemplate are your physical, mental, social, and spiritual health, as these are all intertwined. If you have delayed addressing any of these key components in your life, now is the time to take responsibility to make changes. Take stock of what is important to you, in what priority, and develop your action plan.

Is your physical health where you want it to be? If so, keep up the good work! If not, what will you improve and how? Many new retirees find they have more time to exercise, and this is now part of their daily routine. Perhaps you will have more time to plan and prepare healthier meals. Have you had your annual checkup and discussed with your doctor any aging surprises? Identify and prioritize the issues, then plan your actions.

How is your mental and emotional health? If you have worked with a professional in the past, or are currently doing so, reach out with your questions. If not, it may be time to engage a professional. There are multiple options from retirement and life coaches to therapists, psychologists, and psychiatrists. It is not unusual to experience mixed or new feelings in retirement. Many have discovered that, six months into their new lifestyle, they are feeling a bit let down or depressed. They no longer have the daily demands and routine of work life, they are missing the camaraderie of coffee breaks with coworkers, or they experience diminished feelings of value as their expertise is no longer being sought. This is an opportune time to re-envision what this chapter could look like for you. If you have a partner, address it together and don't hesitate to seek help.

Are you staying socially active? The benefits from staying social can include better health, a brighter mood, better sleep, and staying mentally sharp. Challenge yourself to expand your social circle to meet new friends with common interests, to reach out to old friends and coordinate an activity together, and make time to enjoy your family. Natural communities evolve from a variety of activities like golf, tennis, bocce, pickleball, art classes, book clubs, card games, community gardening, civic and volunteer organizations, and church groups. If you choose to pursue new interests at a community college or a lifetime learning class, you could meet your new friends on this common ground.

What is spiritual health? There are multiple definitions from finding inner peace, to your relationship with God or nature, being your higher self without ego while considering others before yourself, or a journey to living a purposeful life. Spirituality can also be expressed in how you find meaning, hope, and tranquility, and can arise through music, art, and nature. If you have not found what "fulfills" you, then ask yourself these questions:

- What makes me feel most complete?
- What makes me joyful?
- What do I value?
- When am I feeling most connected to others and the world?
- Is it important to me to make an impact on…?

What we do know is that there is a connection between our beliefs and our sense of well-being that assists us in coping with stressful situations.

Perspective, Vision, And Choice

Whether you are preparing to enter the age of retirement or you have already arrived, remember that you are the artist to craft the life you love. You can design your days to seek out new adventures, spend time with friends or family, or offer service to others. How lovely to know that none of these must be exclusive of the others. When you are feeling anxiety or fear of the future, stop and breathe, add your perspective from your wealth of wisdom, and experience, envision your future self in the situation you desire, and choose to move forward and persevere. Just think, you've gotten this far and if you don't like the situation, you can choose to change it!

Here is wishing you a whelm of good fortune and joy.

About the Author

Barbara Archer is a practicing retirement coach at The Retiring Coach and a wealth advisor with HighTower Wealth Advisors. She entered the field of financial services in the 1980s before many women ventured to do so. Barbara has been recognized for her client care by *Forbes*, *Barron's*, and *Worth*. She was honored by the *St. Louis Business Journal* as one of the Most Influential Business Women, and by the YWCA Metro St. Louis Academy of Leaders for Entrepreneurship. Barbara earned her BS and MBA degrees from the University of Dayton and completed Retirement

Risk at Wharton Executive Education Program. She is an investment advisor representative with HighTower Advisors, holding the Certified Financial Planner™, Chartered Life Underwriter®, Accredited Estate Planner®, and Certified Family Business Specialist designations. Barbara and her husband, Steve, enjoy volunteering, golf, travel, and water sports, as well as spending time with their two grown children, Ryan and Kristin. You can reach Ms. Archer at Barbara@retiringcoach.com.

References

Helaina Hovitz, "Some Simple Ways to Turn Anxiety Into Excitement," May 16, 2018, https://greatist.com/live/how-to-turn-anxiety-into-excitement#1

"Carol Dweck: A Summary of Growth and Fixed Mindsets," https://fs.blog/2015/03/carol-dweck-mindset/

Savoring – Making The Fourth Quarter
As Good As The First
By Denise Henry

On a warm summer Saturday afternoon, as a young girl, I made my way to the boarding stable to find my horse at her favorite spot waiting for our usual evening visit. That evening we were headed out for an adventure. Once saddled, I headed to a nearby barn to meet my best friend. Together, we rode five miles down the country lanes on our way to the big event, the local Texas rodeo. Our goal was to get there early so that we could be in the front of the line to enter the grand entrance parade. We were determined to show off our fancy clothes and well-groomed horses, pretending that we were the best of the best cowgirls in town.

Do you have childhood memories like this?

I can vividly remember the aroma of freshly mowed grass from the side of the road and the whinny sounds of horses prancing together as we drew closer to the arena. Yet, what happened at the rodeo grounds that evening is all but gone from my recollection. Those details got lost in the commotion, the lights, and the busy activities swirling around us. We performed, greeted other friends, barely watched the sporting event through scared little fingers plastered on our faces, and then we finally headed home.

Fifty years later, I can still remember that the best part of our journey was on the horseback ride home.

In the gentle breeze of the late evening, two young girls felt free and proud of their accomplishments. We lost sight of the world around us because we were engrossed in our time together doing what teenage girls do. Our chatter focused on highlights of the night, making sure to include all the juicy details while smiling and giggling in the dark all the way home.

Looking back on this memory, I can see we were having the time of our lives. I had no clue that it would be so meaningful to me now, to be able to recount the unique details of our Saturday evening trips to the rodeo. I currently use these precious moments to lift my spirits, reflect on times gone by, and be grateful for my history.

Being able to recall and share these savored moments, now, is something that never entered my mind as a little girl headed to the rodeo. Today, I can tell these compelling stories because I simply have the time to sit back and reminiscence on the savored memories from way back when.

In the fourth quarter of life, there are no guarantees that more moments will continue to show up. Memories may or may not flood our hearts. But, for sure, we can choose right now to be present in every situation that comes our way and show up totally in every event that we purposefully create. If we do not capture the current moments as they happen, we never know when it might be too late.

We are bombarded with messages that say the fourth quarter of life will be the golden years if we have the right financial portfolio. As such, very little information is shared or emphasized regarding the lifestyle choices and planning needs around the nonfinancial aspects of retirement. What is not disclosed in endless financial centered advice are the huge unknown aspects of this vital transition that are not easily understood.

If one is not careful and fully prepared, the things that should bring happiness, joy, and purpose in life will be elusive and hard to find. The good news is what is not understood can be learned.

One of the things we must learn is that we are in the season of life that we must savor. According to author Anna Godbersen, "I've always believed in savoring the moments. In the end, they are the only things we'll have."

You see, savoring is the activity of stepping out of your own experience in the moment to be able to see what is going on, reviewing it, and being able to appreciate the moment as it is happening. It is the difference between hearing the belly laughs -- and being part of them!

Although savoring is usually tied to a good piece of decadent chocolate, a rich yummy glass of wine, or smelling the fresh air just before or after it rains, it can nurture and protect any memorable experience.

One of my favorite times to savor is in the early morning hours as I wake for the day.

Take a minute and think of your morning routine. Could it be something similar? Picture rolling out of bed, with the dawn's breaking light peeking through a slightly drawn blind. Going to the kitchen, you grab your favorite cup of coffee to ease into your day. As you bask in the delicious smells and the warmth of that first cup of coffee, the sensation of comfort and satisfaction grab your attention as you settle into your favorite spot.

Maybe you pick a book to read, delight in a spiritual practice of devotion, or perhaps it is an opportunity to play Sudoku. Now is the time to slow down and relax, keeping your mind away from needless chatter and all the activities that are awaiting your busy day.

What a moment this can be, as you spend this time in appreciation and thankfulness of just being present where you are. Your thoughts expand on how lucky you are to be here. After years of hard work and sacrifice, you notice the outcomes and results that you have achieved. Yes, this is a good cup of coffee.

The act of savoring can change everything – in a moment, and for a lifetime. It teaches you to practice gratitude as well as grace. When you need a positive thought or a loving moment to clear a crazy day, it's there for you in the blink of an eye.

In recalling a great moment with my Mother, I savored it by choosing to be present as the activity was occurring – fully present and soaking in the details as best as possible. It had been two long days in the hospital, not knowing how things were going to turn out. She was transferred by ambulance to a Dallas hospital because the small-town facility did not provide the scope and expertise to diagnose the hidden cause of her heart's unrest. After being poked and tested, she was exhausted to the core of her body. And yet, what she wanted most was a good shower where she could wash off the pain of the sterile environment and the anguish of medical concerns.

That morning, I promised to retrieve her favorite shampoo, hairdryer, and red brush, then style her hair to let her feel a little normalcy once more. After a quick shower given by her nurse, she was sitting up in a stiff leather chair. She was weak from being jostled around but trying her best to be brave through her pain and frustration. I looked in her eyes and asked if she wanted me to still work on her hair, she nodded with a little silly smile and said, "Sure, that would be nice."

As gently as I could, I combed her hair, turned the dryer on to a low temperature, and began the sweet little strokes to lay her white hair down in its most favorite place. She looked up and smiled, telling me how good it felt to have her hair dried while feeling the warm air on her scalp and a gentle massage. At that moment, I realized that I wasn't just drying my

41

Mother's hair, I was telling her how much I loved her and how much I wanted to take away the pain that she was feeling. As I looked down into her eyes, she was absorbed in the relaxing moment and content with where we were. Those minutes, when it felt as if time stood still, became a lasting memory as I saw her sorrow and struggles melt away through a simple act of drying her hair.

We found love carried her through the day and gave her the strength to be released from the hospital to head home. We were together, sharing joy and happiness, even a few happy tears and a little laugh, despite the circumstances.

When I miss my Mom now – because at the time of this writing, it has been one year, two months, and twelve days since she passed away – I instantly recall the tender and rich experience we had in the hospital that day. It was not a grand activity, an expensive gift, or a vacation to remember. However, it was one precious moment in which all that mattered was what we were discovering together.

People don't take the time to slow down and appreciate what they have until they suffer a devastating loss. What loss awaits you during this chapter of life?

Savoring comes when we understand the value of the moment and decide to become present. To be fully present, you have to limit your thoughts to this one moment and nothing else. You must jump right into this moment because nothing else matters –

not right now. The real skill to build is being able to direct your attention without distractions of the busy mind. It is unnecessary to change your thoughts or limit your perspective, but instead shift the focus of your attention on this one thing you are doing and something that you are choosing to magnify. Once the moment is captured, it is time to tuck it away for another day when you have the time to ponder – maybe sipping that next cup of coffee on a cold rainy day.

Learning how to become more present – or mindful if you will – produces a feeling of gratitude and an overall sense of happiness by living fully in that particular moment. From the littlest of instances to the grandest of moments, you can savor each as being equal to the other.

As a child, we moved to a new home almost every year, so the annual challenge was to muster the confidence to enter a new school and make new friends. Finding myself surrounded in a new environment every year once again brought questions to my innocent heart. The silent questions for me to answer were "Who am I?" "What matters most to me?" and "Why am I here?".

Each move took me on an outdoor adventure to ponder those questions. The location I selected was never the same, but the journey was always similar. One time, I ventured into the woods and sat by a still pond. Another time, I remember sitting on the empty bleachers at a baseball field close to the school. And yet another outing, I went into the small-town center to find an inconspicuous bench to sit and get quiet in the hustle and bustle.

My goal was always to take in my new community's scenery, noticing the positive thoughts and feelings that I could capture from deep within my little child's mind. From these locations, I could be more present in my new hometown, right then, in my new place. Why was that savoring? Because it was one quiet, peaceful moment in my changing life that I could purposefully embrace being fully aware in my new space and time. It made me happy to feel grounded in a world that was always moving and changing, knowing that everything would be okay, at least in that moment.

Those same identity questions come up now as the career years have ended. Without my title, without my role, how will I introduce myself? While working and playing all the many roles throughout my career, I felt like I had the answer to who I was. This time of transition into retirement, it makes sense to ask these questions again. Who am I? What matters most to me? Why am I here?

To consciously savor means to be purposeful. For instance, I have found that one of my favorite places to savor is on an airplane, sitting in the window seat. I plan my travel around capturing these moments for a reason. On the way to my destination, looking out on an early sunrise, I can dream about what might be possible for my journey. I use colors in the sky and the clouds already formed to create a story in my mind of all I am hoping to achieve and experience. Likewise, at the end of a long trip, is another great time to savor on a plane. I can put together the story of what happened while watching a beautiful sunset with a view on top of the world.

This time allows me to connect the meaning of my travels and dream about my purpose for the future while sitting in the space of pure awe at the beauty God created on the Earth below.

We were born to savor precious moments when we need to recall something positive because life gets you down or you find yourself suffering. Savoring has helped me through the days when I miss my Mother, lose my true identity, lose my dreams, and feel a lack of purpose. My prayer for you is to go out and savor a meaningful positive experience and add it to your memory bank forever. You never know when you might lose this one opportunity to capture that singular moment ever again.

How will you remember to step out of the moment and capture the picture, image, feeling, or sensations?

You have five senses that can help you become aware of these fleeting moments:

Sound: Notice what the sounds that you hear at this moment are?

Sight: Notice what you see, zoom in on the subject to magnify the details, or expand your eyes view to see the grand image of the environment or the bigger picture.

Taste: Notice what you are tasting or what you imagine tastes of this moment would be.

Smell: Become aware of any pleasant odors and the description you might attach to the aromas.

Touch: Notice what you feel with your hands, legs, and skin, and become aware of all the things that are touching any part of your body.

Bonus Sixth Sense: Notice your body's inner sensations, such as what you notice on the inside of your chest, your heart beating, your lungs expanding with each breath, or your stomach filled with butterflies.

Applying these tips will help you look at the overall picture of what savoring can do for your retirement.

Maybe now is a good time to ask yourself a few questions. Yes, I believe it is the best time. Grab a pen or a pencil and jot down some quick answers, even right here on this page -- answer with less thought and more heart.

Here we go:

- What are the juicy details of the first pleasurable savored experience that comes to your mind?
- What would it be like if you were not able to recall the details of the moments that were so meaningful and treasured?
- How would you feel if you couldn't remember or go back to those times with ease?

- What else can you do to savor your moments in the future?

Some additional ideas to help savor precious moments:

- Take photos.
- Tell someone else your story right after it happens.
- Capture your thoughts, feelings, and gratitude in a journal.

Going forward, what future events or times would you like to put into the memory bank to bring back that special feeling of joy and pleasure?

When we appreciate something, we recognize or pay attention to those things for which we are grateful. However, when we savor something, we take gratitude up a notch by delighting in the quality of the experience and capturing the pleasure in how it makes us feel. The collection of savored moments – of grateful, positive, and honoring experiences – are there for us when we want to relive our happiness over and over again. We spend a lot of time identifying what will eventually make us happy, yet not nearly enough time cherishing and repurposing the things that have already brought us happiness.

At the end of life, when surrounded by your family and friends around your bed, what will be the most cherished moments? Which ones will be the most memorable to your family as you lived the last chapter of your life as one who savors moments?

There is, of course, the other side of the coin. Without being present to savor the moment, there isn't anything to share. A trip to Italy is no different than dining at Olive Garden. The family trip to Greece was no different than meeting up with everyone at the pop-up gyro stand at the State Fair.

As a retirement coach, I understand that what is promised as our golden years may be tarnished. Over the years, we have seen those who have entered into this chapter with nothing but financial foresight being robbed of the moments when they could have built lasting memories by learning to savor. As Godbersen said, in the end, our savored moments are the only things we will have. Everyone deserves to live their best life, to savor the moment, and that includes you. Don't wait.

About The Author

Denise Henry is the founder of Summit Coaching & Consulting, Inc., an organization which helps people design their pre-retirement transitions and supports retirees through the nonfinancial challenges of retirement. Known for her compassionate and truth-telling candor, Denise has coached and trained hundreds of executives and leaders since 2003. Whether working one-on-one with a client or as a group coach, Denise's commitment is to guide people to greater clarity about their vision. Her ability to quickly build trust and her partnering style creates an environment in which others can speak their truth and boldly move to a more purposeful retirement life. Denise is a Certified Retirement Coach and holds an MBA from the University of Dallas. She is a sought-after facilitator and speaker at corporate engagements and various community events. Everyone deserves the formula to the unknowns about retirement; let's get started today. She can be reached at denise@denisehenry.com.

The Key To A Rich Life Begins With You
By Susan Latremoille

When it comes to retirement planning, many focus solely on the monetary side: *How much money will I need to do X-Y-Z once I've retired?*

Money, while important, is only a small piece of the retirement puzzle. To create a fulfilling lifestyle, it's important to also consider the deeper things that bring us happiness and a sense of well-being. This begins with rewiring how we think about retirement.

Rewiring, and not simply retiring, is understanding the opportunity that we have to live life on our terms. Despite what the ads may tell us, there's no such thing as a "cookie-cutter" retirement. The retirement lifestyle that we want to live begins and ends with us.

While many would singularly define a rich life by the level of one's monetary status, I believe that a more robust definition includes the abundance, depth, and fullness of a life well lived. It's the beautiful tapestry that we create when we combine our vision and expectations with our resources in a way that not only impacts us but those around us as well.

In my book, *The Rich Life: Managing Wealth and Purpose*, I share the following mantra for living a rich life: *Live Well, Give Back, Leave a Legacy*.

Live Well: Choosing your values, understanding what is important to you, and prioritizing your life in a way that helps you maintain balance.

Give Back: Finding meaningful ways to contribute to your community.

Leave a Legacy: Impact future generations by leaving a personal mark that represents your life and purpose.

This mantra is a great reminder that our retirement years provide a blank canvas for us to do more.

Before becoming a retirement lifestyle planner, I spent 35 years as a financial advisor. During that time, I had the opportunity to work closely with a number of clients transitioning into retirement. I saw firsthand how their planning (or lack of planning) beyond the financial side impacted their peace of mind long-term.

One client who comes to mind was a busy CEO who meticulously planned for the financial side of retirement, but didn't create a daily plan beyond the generalities of trips, golf, and relaxation.

He planned an African safari for his family after retirement, but didn't give much thought to anything else. After the trip, they rented a condo in Florida for the winter, where they relaxed, soaked up the sunshine, and played golf.

When spring came, and he was back in the city to review his portfolio with me, his demeanor had changed. He was despondent and looked miserable. I didn't recognize the once confident CEO and wondered what could have caused such a drastic change. He admitted that he'd embraced the traditional ideas of retirement, but realized that there was more to retirement than just having enough money to do what you want.

Traditional ideas surrounding retirement have created a false narrative for unsuspecting retirees. Instead of focusing on the lifestyle of retirement and what that entails, we are nudged to place a monetary value on specific activities like golfing, traveling, or volunteering. We then work tirelessly in our careers to make sure that we have enough padding in the nest so that we can feel secure when it's time to take flight.

A life of leisure, while novel, can get old if there's nothing meaningful to fill in the gaps and our vitality can suffer.

This is where I can come in to help clients "rewire not retire" by helping them reshape how they view retirement. This enables them to create a lifestyle that expands beyond traditional expectations and invites a deeper, more fulfilling life experience to unfold.

The concept of "rewire not retire" is not a new one. Many retirees who begin with the best intentions find themselves staring into the bottom of an empty bucket list and wondering what's next. They learn the hard way that retirement is not just an end goal, but it is a new beginning which offers the greatest benefits to those who transition into retirement with a fresh perspective and willingness to embrace change.

Putting The Pieces Together

When you come to the end of a lifelong career and begin to consider how you want to spend your retirement, it's not uncommon to feel unprepared. Business owners and those who've spent years nurturing their careers, can feel especially vulnerable moving into retirement. Plan B is not often on the top of a person's mind until making a decision becomes a necessity.

Just like parenting or starting a business, there is no manual to tell you how to get your retirement just right. However, it is possible to extract the wisdom of life's experiences to formulate a strategy that will get you from where you are today to what you want your retirement to look like tomorrow.

The Rich Life Begins With You

There are as many versions of a rich life as there are people because a rich life is not a one-size-fits-all concept. It's a quality of life that can only be defined by the one who envisions it. Below, we'll explore the many layers of a rich life and how you are the key to creating one with impact during your retirement years.

A Bird's-Eye View

I learned about living a rich life from my father – not by his words, but through his actions as I watched him build a legacy of love and community. He began his career at an early age and continued to build his legacy throughout the length of his adult life. By doing so, he gave me a solid foundation upon which to follow a compass guide for my own life.

My father grew up in Austria in the early 1900s. It was a time of great cultural affluence, and he – along with other members of his family and community – reaped the benefits of their social status. He had the freedom to choose his career path. As a great lover of nature, he chose agricultural school with aspirations to become a farmer.

Although he completed agricultural school, he had to flee the country before Hitler invaded. He never abandoned his dream to farm his own land, so he continued to take steps toward that vision in his new home country of Canada.

Despite the inherent challenges my father faced, he not only fulfilled his desire to become a farmer, but he also became a professor of philosophy. Later, he fulfilled his ultimate dream of running a successful summer camp for boys, which he founded in 1947. To this day, it continues to impact a community of youth.

My father, along with many others who found the secret to living a rich life, had one thing in common – they had an innate understanding of what moved them to take action, and committed to following that lead no matter the cost.

The Rich Life: A Personal Discovery

I began my career as a financial advisor in the 1980s, and although this was my ideal job, the journey to my "perfect fit" was a winding one.

Despite my father's focus on following his dreams, like many girls growing up in the 50s and 60s, I was encouraged to seek "women's work" like teaching or secretarial school. The underlying thought was that I would eventually get married, raise a family, and have a full-time career as a homemaker and housewife.

Against my father's wishes, I enrolled in university. Despite my heart's cry to do more with my life, upon graduation, I settled into the "expected path for women" as a secretary. It was not long before life events brought me to a crossroads, and it was then that I chose to start my own business. It eventually led me into the investment industry – a choice which led to a 30-year love affair with the finance industry.

A life shift was just the push I needed to tap into something deeper and explore new possibilities. I was finally tapping into what my father knew all along, and this was that true wealth comes from the fulfillment of purpose.

Our purpose is defined by the deep desire that we have to connect with the world around us, and I had the pleasure of experiencing this type of reward during my time as a financial advisor. Now, I continue to enjoy the same sense of fulfillment in my career as a retirement lifestyle planner.

The Challenge

When I retired from the financial industry, I had reaped many of the benefits of a fulfilling career, but I also knew that when I retired, I wanted something more.

I had spent years getting to know my clients, their habits, and how money influenced their behavior. Over time, I'd begun to notice that my clients fit into one of two categories. One group used money as a tool to support their dreams, while the other made money become the dream itself.

It's no surprise that clients who used money as a tool found greater happiness and fulfillment in life than those who used the acquisition of money as their only motivator. As I followed many of them into retirement, the effects of their choices became apparent.

How I Got To 'The Rich Life'

In the book, *Happiness: Unlocking the Mysteries of Psychological Wealth*, psychologist Ed Deiner notes the following:

> "Most folks think of wealth in monetary terms, although few people would disagree with the idea that psychological wealth – experiencing happiness and satisfaction due to positive attitudes,

intimate relationships, spirituality, and engagement with meaningful goals – represents a much deeper form of riches."[1]

He goes on to explain how money is only a small part of the larger picture that leads to true wealth.

Similarly, today, I walk clients through the process of "rewiring" how they think about their retirement. Many of us come into retirement with a misguided belief that as long as the monetary side is covered, everything else will fall into place. We envision relaxing on the beach, playing golf at our leisure, and living out our days unencumbered by the daily demands of a career.

In the beginning, the newness of retirement can be exciting. Unfortunately, after the honeymoon phase wears off, if we haven't adequately planned our days, leisurely living can easily turn into long stretches of intense boredom.

If you thrived in a productive environment before retirement, that level of desire for engagement will not suddenly dissipate because your career has come to a close. On the contrary, you'll likely become acutely aware that something is missing.

Fortunately, your life experiences and wisdom give you insight into how to fill that void.

You Are The Key

It's not uncommon to look outside of ourselves when searching for solutions, but in the case of creating an ideal retirement lifestyle, the first steps begin with you.

There are only a few times in life when we're given the opportunity to reinvent ourselves, and our retirement years are one of them.

If you have not given your retirement much thought beyond the financial side, there are several ways I recommend uncovering your retirement potential.

1. **Journaling (DIY):** Writing down what you want your retirement to look like is a great place to start. This will allow you to turn vague thoughts into action steps so that you can move closer to your vision.
2. **Visioning Exercises (DIY):** In the opening of this chapter, I asked you to imagine your ideal retirement. Our subconscious minds respond to visual imagery as if it were real. Take the time to visualize your retirement. No dream is too big. What do you do every day? How do you feel? In what activities do you find your greatest joy?
3. **Ask a Friend (DIY):** Often, our friends can offer great insight into our character that we are unable to see. Ask 10 friends to write you a letter telling you about yourself and their advice to you in retirement.

4. **Assessments:** When you want to go deeper to uncover those areas that move you to take action, then a professional assessment is a good investment. After all, your retirement years are just as important, if not more so, than your career choice. Getting it right at the onset will save a lot of missteps down the road.

5. **Professional Retirement Lifestyle Planning:** Retirement lifestyle planning offers the opportunity to put all the pieces together. A professional retirement planner will work with you to create a strategy for your retirement that looks at the "whole" you, and what will best fit your unique needs.

Assessments And Retirement Lifestyle Planning

Journaling, vision exercises, and asking friends to write letters are excellent ways to scratch the surface of lifestyle retirement planning, but if you want to delve deeper into your behavior and how that could impact your retirement, then professional lifestyle planning is the next step.

When I was in the planning stages of my rewirement, I knew that I wanted to work in the area of retirement coaching, planning, or consulting. As a financial advisor, I'd worked with so many clients over the years who were approaching retirement age and saw how, for many, it was a hit or miss approach. On deciding I wanted to help them, I knew that the first thing I needed to do was to help myself.

In my search for tools to help me better define the specific motivators that informed my choices in life, one of the tools I came across was a unique behavioral assessment test created to collect data from high performers and identify unique traits as strong indicators of success they would be most likely to achieve in their specific areas of life.

When I took the SuccessFinder assessment, I was stunned to find that it not only confirmed many of the character traits I already knew about myself, but it also revealed new insights that I hadn't expected.

The SuccessFinder tool is based on collected data from high performers and the traits that they share. Originally designed to help human resources departments in their recruitment process, these unique behaviors are strong indicators of success in specific areas of life. When moving into retirement, the SuccessFinder tool can predict with high accuracy the specific areas where clients will find success and happiness.

Much of what I learned personally from this in-depth assessment led to my decision to launch SuccessDNA. I'm so confident in the assessment's ability to assist in the rewirement process that I use it with my clients to help them redefine what retirement will look like for them.

Beyond SuccessFinder, I also offer a number of tools to assist with the rewiring process. From quizzes and visioning exercises to one-on-one support, each one has been carefully selected and designed to provide my clients with a concrete roadmap toward personal discovery.

Whether you are planning for retirement or already have both feet in, you are the key to retirement success. The traditional ideals and images of living a life of leisure and sailing off into the sunset don't work in real life. Just as building a career took time, building a retirement that provides more than just a monetary safety net takes careful planning and a deep understanding of who you are and what matters most.

It's never too late to design a personally fulfilling retirement plan – one that offers the freedom of choice, but also adds meaningful substance to your days.

Life doesn't stop after retirement. It continues to move forward whether you are an active participant or not. Your perspective and life experience matter and can positively impact those around you, even during your retirement years.

Discovering the richness of a life well-lived is always worth the effort. Why not begin the rewirement process today by downloading my *free* guide, *Rewire, Don't Retire!: 10 Steps to Your Rewirement Freedom* on my website at www.SuccessDNA.ca.

About The Author

Susan Latremoille spent 35 years of her career as a wealth advisor assisting clients to plan their financial futures and manage their wealth. Witnessing the pitfalls of retiring without a life plan prompted Susan to "rewire" herself as a lifestyle retirement planning advisor. Susan founded SuccessDNA to "help Baby Boomers rewire not retire". She is a partner in Next Chapter Lifestyle Advisors - a venture that works with the financial industry to offer non financial lifestyle advice. Susan is the author of *The Rich Life – Managing Wealth and Purpose* and *It's Not Just about the Money – The Whole Life Approach to Wealth Management*. Susan is a certified SuccessFinder practitioner, holds an MBA and ICD.D (Institute of Corporate Directors) Susan is a graduate of the Family Enterprise Advisor (FEA) program from The Family Enterprise Exchange. Susan is a mother, grandmother, yoga teacher (500 hours), and avid vegetable gardener. She loves to kayak at her summer cottage and cross-country ski in the winter. Find Susan at www.successdna.ca or susan@successdna.ca.

References

Ed Diener and Robert Biswas-Diener, *Happiness: Unlocking the Mysteries of Psychological Wealth*, Malden, MA: Blackwell, 2008.

Life's Continuum: Staying Open To The Unexpected
By Debbie Mitchell

Many of the individuals I've worked with are uncomfortable about not having a precise plan for the next period of their lives. The purpose of this chapter is to remind those of you going through these life, career, or retirement transitions that it is okay not to have all the answers. In fact, staying open to unexpected possibilities and surprise elements often brings about the best and most fulfilling options and life changes.

There are three things I ask clients to consider and I'll ask the same of you. First, be open to thinking "different." In other words, be willing to step back and examine long-held ideas, viewpoints, and perspectives that might not be so relevant or helpful today as you consider where you are heading next. Constraints, often work-related, that may have held you back before may also no longer exist. Putting aside old perspectives will allow you to evaluate more clearly the new. Suddenly, your options have grown exponentially. The window is open. Now what?

Second, there are personality assessment and survey tools available that help you get back in touch with who you are. You may have taken a few of them through the years: Hogan, Birkman, StrengthsFinder, Myers-Briggs, and the like. Pick one and take it again. I can assure you these reports can give you clues to long-forgotten interests that you may have put aside in pursuit of career and family. And while you may believe you know yourself, there is more to discover. A Harvard research program on self-awareness revealed that although 95 percent of people think they're self-aware, only 10 to 15 percent actually are.

Third, if you are waiting for that moment of perfect clarity before you move forward, you may be waiting for it this time next year or in five years. There is seldom 100 percent clarity on anything. Instead of chasing epiphanies, try something now; move forward knowing you've done some solid homework and let that be enough. To borrow a popular phrase (or two), just do it. See how you like it and if it works for you. And if it's not right, fail fast and move on to the next.

Don't expect perfection the first time out. It can be counterproductive and leave a lot unexplored.

Point One: Be Open To Thinking Differently

My guess is that you can create a list of things you're doing right now, or a list of things you are not doing right now, that probably don't coincide with the plan you had going into 2020. And who wouldn't find this disparity in 2020? It's been a year that has required extreme flexibility and agility from all of us. I would also forward the notion that these things have been a mix of the good and the bad, the uplifting and the disheartening.

This move to your next chapter has some similarities. So, while you are moving down an unmapped path, be open to side ventures and new experiences and people. Consider the new, the fresh, the uncomfortable, and the unexpected. Hold back from what might be an immediate impulse of saying "no" to the unexamined and instead ask, "Why haven't I considered this?" or "What might I be missing here?"

Lead with questions instead of shutting down with immediate answers like "I don't like it," "I've already tried it," "It won't work," and "I will fail." Stop. The deeper you've settled in or the longer you've had a belief, the harder it is to hold back and reconsider. Awareness of the fact you just might be shutting yourself off is a major step forward in the process.

As a career and retirement coach, I've seen people start a transition in one place and find that life had some very different, unexpected things in store for them. The following stories represent those of clients, friends, and colleagues that share several themes in common, including being open to considering and trying new things.

Bob is a professional artist today. He wasn't always. I met him over 30 years ago when he ran a corporate annual report strategy and design business. He sold that business, retired from that world, and began to create and build Art Deco furniture. And when his auto racing hobby eventually ended (no worries, now his hobby is flying and he performs aerobatics for his thrills), he transformed that passion to a business creating paintings of collectors' automobiles.

Bob told me that, while he couldn't have predicted where he is today, he works to remain open to new things and always tries to give new ideas total consideration. However, once he decides to do something, he goes after it expecting to succeed at the highest level. He noted that during his life, he has always had a direction, but never felt locked into anything. He also begins to form Plan B and isn't afraid to walk away from something when it's run the course or is no longer working.

Dianne retired from leading a Fortune 100 company's community affairs department to a period of transition. And that transition has kept her very busy. She dropped the need for control that had always been an important part of her approach to life and opened the door to trying new and very different things.

For example, she started doing yoga as strength and agility training. The fact yoga touched on mind, body, and spirit was a perfect fit for Dianne. She began exploring ways to share what she was learning; forming ideas around how to take yoga and its related concepts to others. Today, what was initially a health and wellness hobby has turned into a working concept around children's yoga and restorative programs for teachers.

Dianne noted she used a process of exploring past avocations, and she thought about what had made her the happiest in the past. She looked at what she was doing in those moments, who she was with, and the common elements linking those occasions. The exercise also helped her think in terms of how she wanted to create value in the world beyond the work environment, how she could spend more of her time being of service, and leaving the world a bit better.

Shelley's approach has always been to continuously try new things. She's someone with a long list of interests in so many of life's categories. Today, as a former corporate executive, she's leveraging her strengths: pursuing her interests in writing (off to a Cambridge University graduate degree program this fall), fulfilling her passion for entrepreneurship through advising early-stage companies, co-founding a strategic design practice, and continuing her work as an artist (creating pieces from found objects, new, old, and recycled materials).

Open and curious, relentless, and confident, are traits that have allowed Shelley to explore unexpected new opportunities and keep moving forward. She recalled a sentiment she heard once: Failure is not a tattoo; it's a bruise. She explained she's not afraid of getting some bumps and bruises on her journey! And while she has guardrails regarding the path she's on, there is not a specific plan; her desire is to remain as open as possible to new possibilities.

Bill and Dorothy were married more than 60 years. I admired these two 90-year-olds for their upbeat viewpoint on life, their engagement in learning and the world, the positive affirmations they generously give to others, and their humor. Dorothy, one of the first master's level female chemists in the country, later earned a master's degree in counseling, and began a new career in the mental health world. She continued to engage in educational opportunities until her death. Bill, also a chemist who worked for Union Carbide, continued to take on-line courses in high level math and physics well into his 90s, play the piano, and debate politics.

Again, the common element here is openness. The ability to take input from many different sources, examine it, consider it, and perhaps even try it. But "no" is not the first word that comes to mind for these people. It doesn't mean that everything works for them or that they are indiscriminate in their approach, their values, and their desires. It just means that an open mind and an open heart lead the thought process.

Oh, note that age hasn't dominated the conversation here. These individuals range in age from 58 to 93, but who's counting? Age only becomes relevant when it impacts the body's ability to do something and that's different for everyone. Just for encouragement, I'll reveal that it's the 84-year-old doing the aerobatics.

Some other things to consider as you work to stay open:

1. Just because it didn't work the first time doesn't mean it won't work now. Having thoughts about going back to something you tried once, but in an effort to avoid "failure" you're hesitating? Hopefully, you learned something from the first-time experience. But don't get hung up on the past.
2. Get back in touch with your old interests that other obligations like work and family may have stymied in the past.
3. There are thousands of leisure activities in the world, but you can't seem to find one that interests you. Are you really researching, networking, or trying? I recommend jumping on your laptop and just start googling. I have a fun exercise that lists over 150 leisure activities! It's surprising how many participants have forgotten about.
4. Start looking at "bucket lists." There are bucket list books, blogs, and articles for inspiration.
5. Reread above. How about answering with something other than "no" if an idea is outside of your comfort zone?
6. Practice gratitude, positivity, and intentionality every day. Write down a reminder somewhere if it helps create a habit!
7. You are uniquely you. You don't have to put on the corporate costume anymore. Be vulnerable.

8. Read some books dealing with life transitions, spirituality, health, and wellness, that you would never have read before. Don't put them down until you've made it through. And then ask yourself to produce at least one takeaway regardless of how you felt about the book overall.
9. Allow yourself the time to think about purpose. What can you bring into your life that adds new purpose or reignites an old passion?
10. And finally, take age out of the discussion. After all, it is just a state of mind once you put aside the government-driven benefits qualifications. I suggest we drop worrying about doing something because it is or is not age appropriate, or perhaps you're concerned about the length of remaining life runway. Just authentically be who you are and want to become.

To quote Yoko Ono, "Some people are old at 18 and some people are young at 90. Time is a concept that humans created."

Point Two: Consider Using An Assessment Tool

Personality assessments can highlight your primary needs, both conscious and preconscious, as you consider new ideas, options, and choices for your future. They can increase your self-awareness. Self-awareness is how an individual consciously knows and understands their own character, feelings, motives, and desires.

There are several good assessments available but for retirement or transition coaching, I use the Birkman as it will give you a new look at your usual or strengths behaviors, working style, and motivational needs. The Birkman assessment is non-judgmental, empowering and gives a "beyond the surface" look at ourselves with records and data on 8 million-plus people across six continents and 23 languages.

As you begin to drill down and really consider your interests and style revealed by an assessment, you can begin to think about how they may be translated into specific activities and interests going forward. Will they translate into a new business, working at a nonprofit or start up, volunteering at an organization, and taking courses that you never considered before? Will you start reconsidering some old behaviors that might not be optimal for the personal engagements in your life today? Assessments can be thought provoking and, more importantly, eventually point out new paths, or simply validate and build personal confidence relative to a direction you're already being pulled toward.

Point Three: Don't Wait For Total Clarity

Delay at your own risk! A few years ago, my husband and I decided it was time to seriously downsize. In the basement, we had what had been our "wine cellar," and I use that in loose terms. Cleaning out our stock of wine, it soon became apparent to me that there really wasn't much left there that was drinkable. I pulled out a pinot noir and a white sauvignon, one was dated 2008, and the white, 2012. I found two bottles of my favorite, received as gifts from a friend in California. My idea was to save it for something special; for a time when it would truly be appreciated. Ugh, this was out of date too, and past its drinkable time.

Where did those years go? How could I have forgotten those bottles and missed their drinking years? Five years, then ten years? We had planned to have events, parties, and get-togethers, and knew they would be used.

As I carried the bottles out to be thrown away, I was thinking about how many other things I've been "saving" – things I said I'll do someday, waiting for a better time or for when I would have more information and better clarity. How many other things are there you may be stewing about that are really meant to drink now?

So, don't procrastinate – after all, clarity is really a continuum of sorts. This thing I am calling clarity is organic, ever changing, and never perfect. In the clarity continuum, you start at a place in a situation where you feel unfocused and unsure. Then, through new pieces of information, new insights, and experiences, you can reach a clarity that allows you to move forward. You're ready to take a calculated risk.

Gaining clarity takes action in the form of exploration, research, self-assessment, and reflection, and talking and networking with others. Conduct a cost-benefit analysis. Track your processes and the insights you gain. But know that you'll never know it all. Do the work to know enough. And then simply try it. Don't let anxiety and fear of the unknown be roadblocks. And notice, that as you take those action steps and begin actually doing something, you may find you're starting all over again at some point. Go back and do the work to get enough clarity to modify and recalibrate your direction. But don't let the powerful force of inertia and analysis paralysis prevent you from moving forward.

Hearing the stories of and working with individuals moving through dramatic life changes is terrifically rewarding. It's a privilege to pass along some of the connective tissue that I've seen, experienced, and learned. As you retire from one way of life and move to the next, new, and unexpected opportunities are going to come your way. Remain open to the world – engaged and intentional. I've seen the ultimately rich and rewarding options that will inevitably arise.

About The Author

Debbie Mitchell is an executive, retirement, and career coach, and communications consultant. She helps individuals gain the clarity and focus to identify and achieve their critical objectives. Working toward her ICF accreditation, she has Birkman, Hogan, StrengthsFinder, Marshall Goldsmith Stakeholder Centered Coaching and Retirement Options certifications, and is a graduate of Coach U.

She began coaching in 2017 after a long career as a global communications and investor relations executive for companies including Cardinal Health, L Brands, and Wendy's. Today, she coaches for organizations including Crosworks and Robert Gregory Partners. She can be reached at debmitchellcomms@gmail.com.

References

Tasha Eurich, "What Self-Awareness Really Is (and How to Cultivate It)," *Harvard Business Review*, January 4, 2018.

A Life ReLaunched
By Jan Foran

Every beginning starts with an ending. Sometimes the ending is sudden and unexpected. At other times, the ending occurs after a slow, yet steady journey marked with occasional hills successfully scaled, resulting in a sense of accomplishment. The road then flattens, and the ride continues along a steady pace with only a few minor bumps along the way. Then something happens. For some, this is a gradual awareness of increasing discontent. For others, this is a sudden and dramatic change much like the rug being pulled from underneath. Regardless of circumstances, inevitably we all arrive at this intersection between our familiar present and a cloudy future. Recognizing the signs leading to this intersection and preparing for your transition will provide greater clarity and confidence as you pursue what lies ahead.

I entered into my ReLaunched life as a retirement coach. I did not make this decision suddenly on the day I retired. My journey to this place began seven years before that date. The five years leading to my retirement was a time when I became disenchanted within the work environment. I worked hard to remain energized and engaged. "Lord, help me make it through the day," became my morning prayer. I focused on identifying projects where I could employ my coaching skills to avoid the retired-in-place syndrome. Thus, I was planning for not only my financial readiness to retire; I was planning for my holistic readiness to retire. Along the way I spoke with numerous individuals who have entered their final years of their careers and I found many share very similar feelings to mine. This is what has led me to the Lives ReLaunched project.

For Lives ReLaunched, I interviewed a number of individuals, exploring the environment, events, and feelings they experienced approaching their individual intersection between their lives at work and the journey they chose to follow afterward. We talked about how they embarked upon a different path as well as what their lives are like today. What follows are their stories compiled into a single narrative combining their unique experiences. These individuals gradually became aware of a need to change. They shared with me their lessons learned as they launched into new lives apart from the traditional workplace. I introduce you to Elizabeth.

Elizabeth, Company Executive

I loved my work and the career I created. I worked for someone I greatly respected. We could be completely honest with each other and working for him was actually quite fun! I was encouraged to use my strengths in organizational change and development, training and communication style. As fun as my career was, I noticed over the last five years of my employment an increase in stress. Expectations were changing and ultimately the leader I worked for left the company. Furthermore, this new Vice President did not share the same vision as I for my role.

Gradually, I noticed a change both externally by those on the leadership team and internally with how I felt physically and emotionally. My recommendations seemed to fall on deaf ears, expectations changed, and the resulting work stress along with disenchantment increased as did my sleepless nights. I was so busy I don't know how I managed. I discovered that I no longer enjoyed the corporate life. I am not a morning person and with each and every day I found going to work became a greater struggle. Every morning I woke up with a knot in my stomach. I realized that I was disengaging from the career I once loved and longed for something different.

At one point, I felt so exhausted that I decided to attend a week-long wellness retreat where I learned to meditate. I found that this new practice elevated my self-awareness and that there was nothing left within me to give to the career that I cultivated for the past thirty years. I knew then that for my own overall well-being, I needed to change, and I began to imagine a future away from a familiar, habit-formed world of work.

I started to really plan for what this post corporate life might look like. I recall the disparate feelings I experienced. Imagining where I would go next involved saying goodbye to a familiar life, lifestyle, and social circle. The thought of this was scary. There is comfort in knowing what the next day will look like. Then, I envisioned the adventure that lies ahead in this new reality.

I dreamt of moving out of a house that required a lot of maintenance into a different home. I would be able to travel and visit family living on opposite coasts. Perhaps too I would be able to rediscover enjoyment sharing my work-related strengths on various boards of directors or even start my own consulting business. This process of imagining what the future possibilities could be, caused me to realize what it was about my corporate career that I wanted to take with me into this next stage of my life and what I wanted to leave behind. I wanted – indeed needed – to receive not only validation, but also to realize my influence in affecting positive change in others' lives.

Fortunately, my husband and I did our financial homework and discussed over the course of the past five years our financial readiness for our retirement. Even so, my chronological age had not caught up to my emotional level of retirement readiness. Putting this off would mean greater monthly income from Social Security. Would the cost to my emotional wellness be worth the additional income? Even scarier is the realization that the future paycheck, if there is one, will be smaller. Maybe I can hold off packing up my briefcase and put this retirement thing off a little bit longer.

A year prior to my actual retirement, my husband began to experience serious health issues and I was diagnosed with a medical condition that required a significant lifestyle change. These events caused me to realize I needed to embark on a new journey sooner rather than later.

I knew that I wanted to stay active and I started searching for my next opportunity. I just did not know what that would look like. Initially, I started looking at franchises. I looked at so many of them – even a franchise that sells franchises. I ended up exploring this avenue for three years before realizing that it wasn't for me and that I needed something in which I could create my own offerings.

I decided that if I am to venture out on my own, why should I have to charge exuberant fees and pay another company for something I was skilled in doing? Would you believe it took me three whole years to come to this realization? I wasted so much time and so many resources! This was due to my uncertainty and lack of real direction which also caused me to feel isolated and eventually desperate to nail down the right path for me to pursue, not because I had to, but because I really wanted to.

Ultimately, I created a business focused on training, developing and coaching emerging leaders which has created within me a sense of accomplishment and purpose. It is so amazing to see an emerging leader come into his or her own as a result of the work they have done with me! In addition, I am serving on a couple of non-profit boards where I am successfully influencing strategic direction which aligns with the strengths I developed in the corporate world. I am finding real satisfaction in this new life I launched into. My one regret is that it took so long for me to get from there to here. I would have greatly benefitted from partnering with someone to help me crystallize my experiences into an overarching future vision more quickly.

There were a few surprises along the way as well. I was accustomed to living within a six-figure income and buying anything and everything that I wanted. In fact, my hobby while I was working was shopping. I called it shopping therapy since this is what I did to address my unhappiness in my professional work life. I never paid close attention to my banking accounts because I always had the money.

During the three-years immediately following my retirement, I found out rather suddenly that my spending habit was getting out of hand when the ATM would not give me the cash I requested. Fortunately, I had enough in savings to cover the insufficient funds, yet it was such a rude awakening. I then began to feel as if I never had enough money to do what I wanted to do. However, I learned that I really could survive on less.

While I never worried about balancing my checkbook when I was employed, I learned that I need to pay much closer attention to it in my retirement. Now I have scheduled a weekly money date to make sure I have the funds in the right accounts to pay all of my bills. I also found that living on a reduced income means greater awareness about what I do not have when I am around my wealthier, still-employed friends. When I am with them, I feel more insecure which also surprised me. Of course, this has to do with me comparing myself and my current lifestyle with theirs and while I know they are not judging me, I cannot help but feel envious of them.

Another surprise for me was how important technology would become. I am not proficient when it comes to computers, applications, etc. In fact, my administrative assistant spoiled me by making sure my work computer was turned on and calendar printed out each and every day before I arrived at work. The very first thing I learned when I retired was that no one was going to do that for me! So, when I wanted to establish my home office, I found that I didn't have a clue what to do. This was not my skill set and I was never really interested in technology.

As I look back at this now, I would have better prepared myself as this was a much bigger challenge for me than I had anticipated. I actually called my former administrative assistant seeking help and she simply laughed saying, "You're smart, you can figure it out!" Reality is that being smart is a completely different skill set than the one that requires me to figure out how to deal with technology!

Perhaps the greatest challenge I face is supporting my husband as he faces a debilitating health condition that has no cure. My time with him is precious and so far, we have been able to effectively manage. I have learned that setbacks do occur. Not long ago, my husband experienced a terrifying seizure requiring hospitalization. I am so thankful I was there and, in a position, to truly advocate for him with the hospital administration and physicians. And I am not a spring chicken either! Those years of running marathons are making themselves known. I now walk and hike rather than run. I am looking into yoga and tai chi classes. In a way, this seems like a metaphor for this new life I am leading. I have accepted the fact that it is okay to slow down and smell the flowers, enjoy the mountains and really notice the sunsets.

Overall, I feel that the new life afforded me in retirement has been a wonderful gift. Previously, I felt as if I was working so fast and doing so much that there was so little time to be leisurely. Now I can just sit and reflect upon my life and not have to worry about being late for a meeting. Time has just been one of the greatest gifts to enjoy especially after balancing a career and a family.

I love having the time to incorporate healthy practices like daily visits to the gym and exercising. I love having the time to read a good book that is not work related. I love enjoying a big cup of coffee in the morning and writing in my gratitude journal. I love that I have reconnected with my religion and am growing spiritually. I realize that I have a blessed life and that my glass is overflowing. I know that there will be health challenges to overcome in the future, specifically for my husband and eventually for me. That comes with aging. What is important to me is to navigate this part of my life in a way that is purposeful and provides for me overall happiness and this is where I am currently at. Was it worth it for me to retire when I did? Absolutely!

What We Learn From Elizabeth

Read the Tea Leaves

Elizabeth's story is similar to many others where recognition arises as early as five years prior to leaving a long-standing career. In this case, a cultural shift within the organization left Elizabeth feeling less valued and aware of her growing dissatisfaction, leaving her drained emotionally and physically. Still she continued to work and discovered that her dissatisfaction would not dissipate, even after acknowledging during a wellness retreat the need for change. The tipping point that led to her decision to "pack up her briefcase" occurred when her husband suffered a health emergency.

While not all retirees share the same experiences as Elizabeth, I have talked with a number of retirees who recall similar experiences as they were nearing the end of their careers. Careers provide for us validation for a job well done, and we find within these careers a sense of purpose for our work. What happens when these are compromised? If nothing else self-esteem and overall job satisfaction take a hit. Emotional and physical health becomes compromised. If this sounds like you, then it may be time to consider your options and then.....

Create A Vision; Plan Your Route

Like many of us, Elizabeth and her husband prepared themselves financially for the day they would both be retired. She also planned to apply her skills and talents in her new life. While she secured positions on some non-profit boards, she still took three years exploring franchises before discarding that path for one that led her to developing her own business. Elizabeth felt that she would have benefitted from working with a partner or coach who could help her better create her vision along with a plan for achieving her new goals.

Similarly, others contemplating their retirement begin planning by experimenting with part-time opportunities prior to fully relaunching their new life. Such planning is enhanced where companies provide reduced or flexible work schedules to support their aging workforce.

What is key is understanding your sense of purpose. In his article, "How Will You Measure Your Life", Clayton Christensen writes, "having a clear purpose in my life has been essential," and "I apply my knowledge of the purpose of my life every day. It's the single most useful thing I have ever learned."[1] If you have not yet taken the time to explore what your sense of purpose might look like when you retire, now is a good time to begin.

Expect Some Surprises & Embrace Them!

While Elizabeth and her spouse felt financially prepared for retirement, they both soon learned the value of also planning to change habits. With a six-figure income, Elizabeth rarely felt the need to live according to a budget. She was able to buy whatever she wanted, and she used shopping therapy to treat her stress. It took the shock of insufficient funds to force Elizabeth to change and embrace a new habit of creating a weekly date with her finances.

Elizabeth also embraced technology, an area of admitted weakness. Her need overcame her reluctance and led her to successfully set up her home office, becoming a regular user of current technology. This was definitely outside of Elizabeth's comfort zone.

Imagine how we too will grow in our knowledge and self-esteem by exploring that space outside of our comfort zones!

As Jonathan Look noted in his article, "The Magic of Leaving Your Comfort Zones in Retirement" "Studies have proven that learning new and demanding things outside of our comfort zones (and maintaining an active social network) is key in keeping us sharp as we age. Merely exercising the mind with things that don't push our boundaries, such as reading or puzzles, doesn't necessarily improve cognitive function. It has to be new things that create a bit of anxiety fub offer potential rewards."[2]

I submit that in addition to keeping ourselves cognitively engaged, the learning we derive outside our comfort zones serves to boost our confidence and strengthen our self-esteem.

Engage In Restorative Practices

Elizabeth acknowledged the impact of health challenges that she and her husband face. She sees these as part of her new reality, which led her to addressing them in a healthy fashion. She has modified her lifestyle to incorporate a healthy diet and appropriate exercise all designed to maintain her overall health. She also addressed her emotional health with a positive outlook and taking time to embrace the moments.

Spiritually, Elizabeth renewed her relationship with her religion and spends time focusing on what she is grateful for. According to Marianne T. Oehser, There is also a growing body of research about the physical and emotional benefits of meditation and prayer. They reduce stress and create a sense of peace and joy. The gift of having more time available to reflect may give you the opportunity to increase your awareness of the present moment – which after all is where we actually live our lives.[3]

Taking a holistic approach to your overall health; the mind, body and spirit will serve to help you develop your resilience as you navigate this transition.

Elizabeth's retirement story may resonate with you. Then again, it may not. Elizabeth exhibited a significant amount of control over the timing of her retirement and she developed a high-level vision of what her retirement would look like. I have interviewed others who experienced significantly different paths, some who had retirement thrust upon them as a result of their own health situations; others were forced into retirement as a result of unexpected unemployment. If these situations reflect your circumstance, or if you have a different story, I would like to hear from you. Please join my contact list by visiting my website, www.successfulshifts.com.

About The Author

Jan is a credentialed coach with the International Coach Federation, a certified Retirement Coach, and holds a master's degree in Administrative Sciences. Jan recently retired from a long and successful corporate career, where she worked in talent management, talent acquisition and human resources. Most recently, she coached individuals at various levels of management on leadership development and organizational effectiveness. Jan is currently applying her leadership development and career coaching talents to help individuals near retirement or recently retired to relaunch their ideal retirement lifestyle. She can be reached at jgforan@successfulshifts.com

References

1. Clayton M. Christensen, "How Will You Measure Your Life?," *Harvard Business Review*, July-August 2010.

2. Jonathan Look, "The Magic of Leaving Your Comfort Zones in Retirement," *Next Avenue*, June 17, 2015.

3. Marianne T. Oehser, *Your Happiness Portfolio for Retirement*, Carlsbad, CA: Balboa Press, 2019.

Fire Drill For Retirement: The COVID Experience
By Pamela Karr

When it comes to retirement, most of us are more concerned about having enough money to spend on our desired lifestyles than we are with how we will spend all our new-found time. Retirement is a major transition, but it goes far beyond its financial aspects. Retirement (defined as leaving one's current full-time employment) is a major life change that impacts every aspect of life, including one's routine, social network, relationship with spouse or partner, sense of identity, and physical and mental health. Ideally, we would spend as much time planning for the nonfinancial side of life after working as we do for the financial side. But how many full-time working professionals have or take the time to plan ahead and to design their next acts? My experience as a retirement coach has shown me that not many do.

During conversations with friends and clients about how they were coping during their stay-at-home experiences during COVID, several jokingly referred to this time as "like being in retirement." At the same time, I noted that one expert was calling this a "fire drill" for retirement.

Was it?

Did suddenly being sequestered at home provide individuals with a glimpse of what it might be like when they stop working full time? Could the experience also provide information about how prepared an individual was to embark upon a post-retirement lifestyle? The topic intrigued me, so I set out to learn more about individual experiences by developing and distributing a survey.

The Survey

My team and I developed a short survey aimed at individuals who self-identified as planning to retire in the next year, or considering retiring within the next five years. The survey took from five to fifteen minutes to complete, depending on how many optional comments a person made. We distributed it to former colleagues, local community members, former high school classmates, and family and friends. If a correspondent fit into the targeted group, we asked them to complete the survey. In addition, we requested their help in identifying other relevant persons who would be willing to complete the survey and supplied a link to it.

The survey was composed of two parts. Part one contained questions about a person's stay-at-home experience and its impacts on routine, social networks, relationships with spouse or partner, interests outside of work, and physical and mental health practices. Part two asked the individual to reflect upon what the experience showed them about their need for structure; the depth and breadth of their social network; the ability to co-exist with their partner on a full time basis; the number of interests outside of work and; the experience's impact on their overall desire to retire.

The observations and antidotes contained in this chapter come primarily from the subset of those respondents who indicated that they planned to retire from their current job within the next year or within the next five years and had worked fewer hours per day than during a typical work week or did not work at all during the crisis. We will refer to this subset as our *target group*. We believe that the respondents in this target group had experiences that more closely mirrored retirement than did those who worked the same number or more hours from home as they had typically worked.

We freely acknowledge that the COVID-19 stay-at-home experience did not truly mirror life in retirement. It is clearly difficult to try new pursuits or join new groups from a distance of six feet, for example! Even so, we hope you will enjoy the following comments and insights from participants about what their stay-at-home COVID-19 experience taught them.

Daily Routines And Structure

One of the things that work provides us, in addition to a paycheck, is structure and routine. If you suddenly have forty or more extra hours a week, that can feel totally freeing – or more than a little disorienting.

We asked our survey participants, "How well did you adjust to the disruption of your usual daily routine?" Out of our target group, an equal number answered "well" or "bumpy at first and then I figured

out how to add the level of structure that I need."
Only a few answered that they "felt
discombobulated the whole time."

Responses to the invitation to elaborate about
adjusting to the disruption of the usual daily routine
included:

- I eventually worked out a schedule consisting
  of reading the paper, exercise, work, food.
  preparation, and of course, a little TV
  watching.
- I found myself eating too much, but enjoyed
  the time to tackle home chores, to read, and
  to go for walks with friends.
- A welcome respite.
- I've actually enjoyed it! Has shown me that I'll
  probably also enjoy retirement.

We also asked our participants, "What did you learn
about your need to add structure to your days?" A
large majority answered, "I need a semi-structured
approach but can easily modify plans." Fewer
persons selected:

"I prefer an easy-going, anything-can-happen
approach," or "I prefer established routines with
checklists."

Comments related to the question above included:

- Need have a "to-do" list, but not bound by
  staying on schedule – everything is much
  more casual.

- If I don't have structure of some type, I fritter my time away on frivolous things.
- I need a list, but am more flexible about how and when the tasks/activities on it get completed.
- And from the person who likes routines and checklists: Structure is good, but I sometimes overrate it.

Now It Is Your Turn: How would you answer the questions below?

How well did you adjust to the disruption of your usual daily routine?

1. Well.
2. Bumpy at first and then I figured out how to add the level of structure that I need.
3. Felt discombobulated the whole time.

What did you learn about your need to add structure to your days?

1. I prefer an easy-going, anything-can-happen approach.
2. I need a semi-structured approach, but can easily modify plans.
3. I prefer established routines with check lists.

Get A Head Start: Do This Before You Retire

My clients vary greatly in their need and desire for a structured and planned lifestyle. I have included a book, *Retire Smart Retire Happy: Finding Your True Path in Life* by Nancy Schlossberg, in the suggested reading list at the end of this chapter. Schlossberg lists five different paths that people use to orient and structure their post-retirement lives as:

- Continuers for whom identity in previous work is still central;
- Adventurers who move in new directions;
- Searchers who are separating from the past but still searching for their place;
- Easy Gliders who are content, enjoy retirement, go with the flow; and
- Retreaters who have given up on forging a new, rewarding life.

The Depth And Breadth Of Social Network

Another thing that work usually provides us is regular contact with others. Almost all the answers to the question, "What did you miss most about being present at your regular place of work?" were related to missing the comradery and interactions with co-workers and clients. Though we often think of our work colleagues as friends, relationships do change once we leave the workplace.

We asked our survey participants, "How connected did you stay with those in your social network – coworkers, family and friends?" Half of those in our target group responded, "I found opportunities to connect more deeply with some in my social network" and the other half chose, "I stayed somewhat connected." Only one respondent indicated that she "felt pretty isolated."

Responses to the invitation to elaborate about staying connected with their social network included suggestions like:

- Had phone conversations with many old friends.
- Walking and talking with friends; texting and calling others a bit more; seeing lots of neighbors and meeting new ones.
- I talked with or texted with my co-workers on a regular basis. Some of them I kept up with on Facebook.
- I found that I reached out to work colleagues and family more often to feel connected as I live alone.

We also asked our participants, "What did you learn about the depth and breadth of your social network outside for work?" Half of our target group answered "I have a strong social network in place (i.e., friends, family, church, volunteer activities, interest groups, and neighbors). Of the others in the group, 30 percent answered, "I will probably focus on deepening relationships within my existing social network," and 20 percent answered, "I will want to work on expanding my existing social network."

Comments related to the question above included:

- I loved reaching out to old friends and family during this time. I will continue to stay more connected with them post retirement.
- Truthfully, it taught me more self-reliance and independence.

- I'd like to continue to meet new people and try new things – like more kayaking, which I tried last year with some women from church!
- After the number of years I had at work, my colleagues were my social network; a few still are. I have children and grandchildren in the area, but want to avoid depending on them entirely for my entertainment. I will be adding volunteer work to my weekly schedule.

Now It Is Your Turn: How would you answer the questions below?

How connected did you stay with those in your social network – coworkers, family, and friends?

1. I found opportunities to connect more deeply with some in my social network.
2. Stayed somewhat connected.
3. Felt pretty isolated.

What did you learn about the depth and breadth of your social network outside for work?

1. I have a strong social network in place (i.e., friends, family, church, volunteer activities, interest groups, and neighbors).
2. I will probably focus on deepening relationships within my existing social network.
3. I will want to work on expanding my social network.

Get A Head Start: Do This Before You Retire

Make a "Friends List." In the first column, list people in various categories such as family, friends, co-workers, and others (i.e., fellow church members, volunteers, neighbors, and professional peers). In the second column, rate the present relationship with each on a scale of 1-5 according to the depth. In the third column, assign a rating of 1-5 to the desired relationship with each. Make time to reach out to selected individuals on a more regular basis prior to your retirement date.

Being Home With A Partner On A Full-Time Basis

The relationship a couple has after retirement is the relationship they have before retirement, only amplified! The issues that exist throughout the marriage/relationship will still be there, but may be harder to ignore with the increased time together.

We asked our survey participants, "If applicable, how comfortable was the experience of being at home full time with your partner?" Half of our target group responded, "we coexisted very well," and half selected, "we had our moments but managed to work it out."

Responses to the question above included:

- Took walks together, stayed out of each other's way when necessary, had separate home offices.

- After 45 years of marriage, I thought we would really get on each other's nerves with so much togetherness but that was not the case.
- We got on each other's nerves, sometimes, but have talked it out successfully.
- He had already been retired for six years and had his routine set.

We also asked our survey participants, "How prepared are you and your partner to thrive in retirement together?" Most of our target group responded, "we are good to go." Only a few responded, "we need to work on some issues and better communicate our individual visions."

Responses to the question above included:

- As long as we both have activities lined up to keep us busy, we'll be good. Our relationship will be fine. The challenge will be for each of us to have a strong calling to pursue new interests – reading, studies, hobbies, gardening, travel, etc.
- We are pretty easy-going people who enjoy a lot of the same interests. We do not have to be together all the time, but usually enjoy our time together.
- He's interested in fly fishing and hunting. I'm not. But we can both do things without each other, and do things together.

Now It Is Your Turn: How would you answer the questions below?

If applicable, how comfortable was the experience of being at home full time with your partner?

1. We coexisted very well.
2. We had our moments, but managed to work it out.
3. Not very well at all.
4. Not applicable.

How prepared are you and your partner to thrive in retirement together?

1. We are good to go.
2. We need to work on some issues and better communicate our individual visions.
3. We have a lot of work to do in order to peacefully coexist.

Get A Head Start: Do This Before You Retire

The key to a healthy relationship is communication. Don't assume your partner feels the same way you do about important issues related to life after retirement. It doesn't matter how long you have been together; relationships are always a work in progress. For a great list of key conversations couples should have before retirement, and wonderful suggestions about how to discuss difficult subjects, we recommend *The Couples Retirement Puzzle: 10 Must-Have Conversations for Creating an Amazing New Life Together*, as listed in the suggested reading list at the end of the chapter.

Interests Outside Of Work

Chances are you wrestled with some degree of cabin fever during your stay-at-home experience. Retirees often experience something similar a few months into retirement. The to-do list is done, the big vacation is over, and suddenly, one morning, the question comes up: What do I do now?

We asked our survey participants, "In general, how easily did you find ways to occupy your time outside of work activities?" Over half of our target group responded, "very easily – lots of projects and interests to pursue." About a third responded, "fairly easily with lots of help from media," with only a couple responding, "not easily – often bored."

When invited to elaborate on their answer to the question above, comments included:

- I've enjoyed getting tasks done that I never had time for previously.
- I did lots of reorganizing at home in the kitchen and bedroom. I also started selling Pampered Chef to help with income and found that I love doing it.
- I have been amazed at how quickly the days go by and how few big projects I've completed.
- Eating, weeding, and reading. Biking and hiking (walking). Cooking and cleaning. Origami! New tennis racket!
- I love gardening, and I enjoyed planting flowers and preparing my yard for summer.

We also asked our participants, "Have you begun to identify meaningful and motivating activities (i.e., part-time work, volunteer work, and interests) to pursue once you no longer work full time?" Half of our target group responded, "I have identified several options and am starting to explore opportunities." The other half were equally divided among, "I have a few ideas but have not had time to explore them;" "I am anxious about what I will do with my time;" and "I am not concerned about finding new activities."

Comments and elaborations to this prompt included:

- I am sure there will be plenty of opportunities to volunteer and keep busy.
- I have some concern that in the winter months I will get bored/lonely, because in the spring and summer I work in my garden a lot. I also worry about eating too much and not maintaining my four-times-a-week YMCA activities.
- We have a home out west, but have not had the time to fully take advantage of it. This experience has made us more motivated to do so.
- I definitely need to cultivate work that involves the creative process with some travel.
- I am looking into an "at-home" business opportunity and some volunteer work.

Now It Is Your Turn: How would you answer the questions below?

In general, how easily did you find ways to occupy your time outside of work activities?

1. Very easily – lots of projects and interests.
2. Fairly easily with the help of lots of media.
3. Not very easily – often bored.

Have you begun to identify meaningful and motivating activities (i.e., part-time work, volunteer work, and interests) to pursue once you no longer work full time?

1. I have identified several options and am starting to explore opportunities.
2. I have a few ideas, but have not had time to explore them.
3. I am anxious about what I will do with my time.
4. I am not concerned about finding new activities.

Get A Head Start: Do These Two Things Before You Retire

1. Start to build a "Curious List" of anything and everything you might want to explore or learn or do someday. You may surprise yourself (as I did when I made one myself) at the number of interests you have. Begin to star items that stand out for you. Hold it for use later as you plan out one of your weeks or months in retirement. Go for quantity. You will need a long and diverse list of activities you might pursue that can last not just for

weeks, or months, but quite likely for decades. I have included a book, *What Will I Do All Day?*, in the suggested readings list at the end of this chapter.

2. Perhaps my favorite book about the retirement transition is *Don't Retire, Rewire* by Sedlar and Minors. The authors focus on helping people identify their "drivers," or personal motivators. Knowing what gives you satisfaction in your working life can help you select future activities that will be the most satisfying and fulfilling to you. We all know what we are retiring "from," but what will you retire "to?" I highly recommend buying this book and completing the exercises within it.

Effect On Overall Desire To Retire

We asked our survey participants, "How has this stay-at-home COVID-19 experience affected your overall desire and plans to retire?" Half of our target group responded, "I am more eager to retire from my current job than I previously was." About a third answered, "I feel the same way that I did before my COVID-19 stay at home experience," with just a couple of people responding, "I am more reluctant to leave my current work behind."

Comments from those respondents who answered that they were more eager to retire included:

- I liked not dealing with the daily hassles of work.
- Perfect timing to make the decision.

- I can figure this out and get a lot out of it.

Comments from those who answered they felt about the same way they did prior to their experience included:

- The timetable to retire and work part-time was pushed up by about a year.
- I figure it is just going to be less of a shock staying at home and going to retirement versus going from the office to retirement.
- I was somewhat concerned about not being able to fill my days, but this experience showed that that was not really the case.
- I had already planned to retire on June 1. I have to admit that I missed the goodbyes and hugs from coworkers that my last day would and should have given me. There was no "formal" end to my 34-plus years with the organization. Very difficult.

Now It Is Your Turn: How would you answer the question below?

How has this stay-at-home COVID-19 experience affected your overall desire and plans to retire?

1. I am more eager to retire from my current job that I previously was.
2. I feel about the same way that I did before my COVID-19 stay at home experience.
3. I am more reluctant to leave my current work behind.

Get Pumped! Spend Some Time Thinking About Your Next Phase of Life Before You Retire

I sincerely hope that reading the responses and comments of others to the questions in the survey and, then considering your own responses to the questions was thought provoking. How prepared are you to enter your next chapter in life?

There is no one-size-fits all retirement. It is up to each person to discern and design their next acts. The list of possibilities for new opportunities, new activities, and new meaning is endless. The transition into retirement is smoother and more enjoyable with a bit of advanced planning.

In addition to completing some of the activities listed in the "Head Start" sections, consider finding time for one or both of the next suggestions.

1. Take part in a pre-retirement workshop. In addition to researching offerings in your area, you may be interested in taking part in one offered virtually. I am currently developing such a workshop to be available in early 2021. If you would like to be notified when the course is up and running, please email me at pamelarkarr@gmail.com.
2. Consult with a certified professional retirement coach. You can find a list of professionals in your area at CertifiedRetirementCoach.org.

About The Author

Pamela R. Karr is a licensed clinical mental health counselor, a national certified counselor, and a Certified Professional Retirement Coach. Two years ago, she retired after twenty-three years as program manager of the Wake Forest University Department of Counseling. The rewired Pamela now provides retirement coaching for individuals and couples, and conducts workshops for businesses and nonprofit organizations. You can contact her at www.linkedin.com/in/pamela-r-karr or at pamelarkarr@gmail.com.

References

Patrice Jenkins, *What Will I Do All Day? Wisdom to Get You over Retirement and on with Living*, Self-published, 2017.

Nancy K. Schlossberg, *Retire Smart, Retire Happy: Finding Your True Path in Life*. American Psychological Association, 2004.

Jeri Sedlar and Rick Miners, *Don't Retire, Rewire: 5 Steps to Fulfilling Work that Fuels Your Passion, Suits Your Personality, and Fills Your Pocket*, Third edition, Alpha, 2018.

Roberta Taylor and Dorian Mintzer, *The Couple's Retirement Puzzle: 10 Must-Have Conversations for Creating an Amazing New Life Together*, Sourcebooks, 2014.

911 Issues In First Responder Retirement
By Jim Hyde

I hit the wall after 31 years of law enforcement. The Great Recession of the twenty-first century had taken a toll on our California city and me. The city was on the verge of bankruptcy and I was the captain (police chief) of a sinking ship. We had already reduced the police department's workforce by 45 percent through layoffs and early retirements. Many of the neighborhoods across our city that we had taken back from crime were now being surrendered back to the criminals.

I was burned out. My wife found me sitting in our living room with a notepad one morning at 2 a.m. trying to figure out new ways to save jobs. I had only slept two to three hours a night for the past year. She could see the fatigue on my face and body. Susan looked me in the eye as I sat there and said, "The job is killing you and I need you to get out, I don't want to be a widow." The second thing that I loved the most, being a police officer, was the thing that was slowly killing me.

I had been in the cardiac care unit a month earlier, for three days, with chest pains and high blood pressure. The cardiologist who discharged me from the hospital said, "I think it's time you find a new profession."

After three decades, I lost 38 of my first responder colleagues to murder, suicide, accidents, and catastrophic medical events. I attended 104 first responder funerals. I spent two-thirds of my adult life away from my family on the mission of protecting other families. It was time to refocus my purpose, passion, and calling in life before the job took my life

Step 1: Refocus My Life

It was also time to fix my tired body. I already suffered eleven broken bones and seven surgeries from work-related injuries. I had also delayed reconstructive surgery on my shoulder for two years to keep working to protect our city. So, I told my city manager that it was finally time to have the surgery to repair my body. I placed my work affairs in order and went on medical leave. While I was off work for two months healing and rehabbing from my surgery, I started exploring what my next purpose in life would be defined as.

I told my wife that I would start the filing process for retirement from policing. I knew that I had more to contribute to the profession. I had been born into a family of overachieving and successful Hyde men. They always reminded me that whatever I did in the world, I had to do something that served humanity. They had been raised in the Depression era and had known nothing but a world at war. The first responder career had met the mark that the previous generation of men encouraged me to follow. It had also given me a proven set of problem-solving skills that could still benefit others. Unfortunately, I soon discovered there was no clear road map or blueprint to find the way to my next new purposeful life.

So, I started the journey to find my "new normal" of a healthy way of living, growing, and achieving. Susan and I began to study the best practices for an active and meaningful first responder retirement. One of our first challenges was learning how we could go from a 120 miles per hour (mph) first responder lifestyle, which we lived for decades, to a 55-mph normal lifestyle.

My wife Susan and I have spent more than three decades working with first responders and soldiers across the country who had been suffering in silence. Five of our law enforcement colleagues had taken their lives due to post-traumatic stress disorder (PTSD). We couldn't just stand by and watch that continue to happen. We had to do something to help the well-being of our first responder and military brothers and sisters.

We had developed a series of nationally recognized trauma recovery programs and best practices designed to help those struggling with psychological injuries. We had implemented these interventions in a variety of ways through training, trauma retreats, peer support programs, and embedded military behavioral health programs around the globe.

Across America, our Spartan guardian brothers and sisters were suffering at alarming rates. For every law enforcement member killed in the line of duty, two to three more took their own lives. On average,

EMTs only last eight years in their careers before they burn out and leave their honorable profession. Firefighter trauma numbers were also going up exponentially.

Step 2: Finding A New Purpose

The three decades I spent as a policeman, including a stint as a police chief in two California cities, seemed only a preamble to the new direction that I was supposed to be going. I started exploring my career options. Because of my education and experience in trauma psychology, I was approached by military friends to enlist in the California Army National Guard and go to Officer Candidate School (OCS) to become a behavioral health officer. They needed help reducing the growing epidemic of soldier PTSD and suicide. The years of fighting the war on terrorism were taking a toll on the limited mental health resources, which happened to be one of my skill sets.

So, I enlisted into the Army National Guard at age 53. I was given an age waiver because of my law enforcement and psychology background. My wife told me that I was out of my mind, but she would support me if I was not deploying to the Middle East. OCS was an applied leadership program. It required an intensive level of performance by officer candidates, more than basic soldier training affords. Basic training teaches recruits to do everything from brushing their teeth to the correct way to sit, stand and march. A great deal of OCS training consists of challenging candidates with a series of complex problems, expecting them to work as a team to solve issues and complete the exercise.

One of those problems, for example, was the Leader Reaction Course (LRC). Recruits in boot camp are faced with an obstacle course consisting of walls, ropes, and running. The LRC obstacle course, on the other hand, combines the basic obstacle course with complicated challenges team members (squads) must solve. Each LRC exercise involves a unique obstacle. In each case, we had to devise some way to get ourselves and our equipment from one side of the "impossible obstacle" to the other. Success always requires teamwork, planning, and communication. Success equals winning and winning equals rewards.

Unbeknownst to me, OCS was giving me a new set of leadership skills and business management tools. I was learning how to lead and build a small business with a clear direction and mission. I thought I had learned a lot as a police officer and police chief, but OCS added another layer of applied planning knowledge and experience.

Nine months later, I graduated from the Army OCS program with the nickname of "Dad". I was given the nickname by my classmates because I was the oldest OCS candidate ever. I was then assigned to the National Guard's Behavioral Health Unit. The unit commander gave me the mission of implementing and growing pre- and post-deployment programs to combat stress.

I was back to being busy, in fact as busy as during my career as a cop. I continued to pursue the passions of service and program building that were an important part of my life during the past three decades of police work. I was part of a team helping reverse the growing impact of PTSD and suicide among soldiers who were deploying to and returning from Middle East battle fields. I was enjoying the work and the challenges of military life, but something in my heart was calling me back to the first responder community.

Step 3: The Birth Of A New Idea

Several years earlier, my wife had started interviewing pre- and post-retirement first responders concerning their transition plans. The Great Recession of 2007 was forcing veteran first responders to retire early to save the careers of younger first responders. The common denominator she found was that, for most, there really was not a plan other than going camping and fishing.

She found that recently retired first responders were struggling in several aspects of their early retirement life. They were suffering with symptoms of anxiety and depression. They told her that they had lost a sense of purpose in life along with a loss of professional identity. Through her interviews and research, she discovered that individuals in high-performing professions place a significant amount of emotion and energy into their identity and status in society.

These recently retired first responders were also struggling with significant health issues that had been left untreated during the last years of their careers. A common trait for the first responder culture is to be strong and push through personal physical and emotional problems. This is done to support the mission of protecting communities and supporting comrades.

Members of the first responder professions, whether currently in uniform or not, differ in fundamental ways from the civilian populations they serve. Those serving or having served in uniform share a similar set of beliefs, attitudes, and behaviors that we can refer to as the "Culture of the Uniform". For the most part, people outside this unique culture are not aware of its existence.

The life-and-death environments that first responders operate in do not allow for many mistakes. The intensity of such expectations leads to continual self-evaluation of performance. At the beginning of a first responder's career, the academies pound the standards of perfectionism and continuous improvement into recruits. This never ceases throughout a career. The low tolerance level for mistakes and errors means first responders are going to continually self-evaluate their performance at many levels.

They force themselves to live by a professional and personal code of conduct that extends beyond mere perfection into the core value of "sacrifice". People in uniform put themselves in harm's way and accept their potential injury or death as an inherent part of the profession. Thus, "protecting" others is another core value of the uniform culture.

Another valued trait of the culture is the expectation of extended absence from home and family. My own career, working patrol, narcotics, gangs, organized crime, and homicide, caused me to spend days at a time away from my family. At one point in my career, it extended past physical absence into emotional absence. Many times, I would be so exhausted when I finally made it home, that I would walk right past my waiting family to the bedroom. I had changed the bedroom into an isolation chamber with aluminum foil-covered windows, so I could get a few precious hours of sleep.

One more valued trait of the culture of the uniform is that of the "warrior mindset" – the mindset that many people and things can be potential dangers. It reinforces courage over fear when confronting potential threats and adversaries. There is a downside. The same warrior mindset that helps first responders stand up to dangers also makes it difficult for them to ask for help, since they believe that doing so would be an admission of weakness. One of our ongoing challenges, therefore, is to help first responders to understand that everyone needs help, at one time or another; that not asking for help when you really need it is not a sign of weakness, but one of strength and courage.

Step 4: The First Responder Retirement Business

First responders are trained and evaluated to be high-performing professionals their entire career. So, when they retire from the profession, they experience significant emotional and psychological changes. *The Harvard Business Review* published an article on the impact of retirement on high-performing professionals. The article stated, "Their life anchors are their identification with an institution of great power; influence over individuals, policies, finances, and the community; and constant affirmation of their importance as individuals and of their role as leaders. With retirement, all these anchors disappear from one day to the next."[1]

First responders are great planners at work, but usually not so great on the home front. The demanding career of a first responder most often comes first and family second. Our own research showed that retirement is a major life event for first responders. For some, it rises to the level of a critical incident. Everything a first responder represented in the world suddenly comes to a quiet end. For the majority of first responders, there is no farewell luncheon or "thank you for your sacrifice and service" ceremony. You are just out the door. Many quietly slip out the back door to avoid the strong emotions evoked with separating from the guardian-warrior culture.

As I learned, the huge first responder locomotive just keeps rolling down the tracks, but you are no longer on it and it keeps getting smaller and smaller as it moves away. Suddenly, you are alone. This newfound loneliness may result in depression and trigger long-buried memories of traumatic experiences. First responders must have a plan to survive and flourish for a truly successful retirement.

Within weeks after retiring from the active first responder community, you go from confident to questioning the decision of leaving your career. After a week, you are almost forgotten by the organization's members. Your former colleagues will wave and say "hi" to you in passing on the street, but you are no longer on the team. The retirement transition can significantly impact your physical, emotional, and mental health. At some point early on, you realize that after pouring out your heart and soul for 30 to 40 years to the first responder mission, you wonder if you actually made a positive difference in the world. The missed family events like birthdays and special holidays cannot be brought back. This is coupled with the significant loss of perceived value and purpose in the world.

For many people, retirement can feel like a form of suspended animation. What I called the "Retirement Grieving Syndrome" (RGS) can develop with the large amount of unstructured time, a sense of idleness, and boredom – and for some, depression. First responders work and sacrifice for decades to get to the retirement prize and, to their surprise, arrive at an unnamed and empty wilderness location called the "unplanned retirement zone". They thought there would be a simple map waiting at the trail head with directions to their dream retirement destination.

Our research showed that key retirement planning steps are essential to establishing a new personal identity and purpose – finding other ways to rebuild that sense of belonging, like the one you had as a first responder. There are other losses to be dealt with, such as the loss of influence and importance. It is a big adjustment.

We also discovered that those first responders who held high ranking positions were most likely to struggle the most emotionally in retirement. They soon learned that the many community member friends they thought they had, were not actually friends – they were people who wanted to be associated with the perceived power and influence of their rank. Being a police or fire chief can be a lonely position and even lonelier in retirement.

Step 5: Finding The Right Business Recipe

Now I had a direction to move in – to build out a first responder retirement education and coaching service. The next problem I faced was that after spending most of my adult life working in government, I had no idea how to start a new business from scratch, let alone grow it into a successful business. I talked to friends, interviewed other small business owners, looked at business management school programs, and researched the web to find business coaching companies.

I was looking for a business education and coaching company that had an ethical track record, was proven to deliver concise and clear business methodologies, and was available when I needed their experience to get past a significant hurdle.

After months of searching, I found the Retirement Coaching Association (RCA). They could show me the secret sauce of future business success. I discovered small business owners and fledgling entrepreneurs like me, looking for their new purpose and path in the world of retirement. I finally found meaningful retirement curriculum. My wife, Susan, and I had attended a semester-long retirement transition course at a local university near our home. It was a good starting place but lacked a lot of detail.

The various RCA business owners and presenters opened my mind to a new world of opportunity. They showed me a powerful way to help retiring first responders create their personal retirement lifestyle blueprint for the next two to three decades of their lives. My wife and I could now build a business system to significantly reduce first responder post-retirement depression, divorce, and suicide. We would be saving the lives of the lifesavers again!

Step 6: Saving 'The Lifesavers'

Today, we work with pre- and post-retired first responders who don't have a clear direction for their retirement. These purpose-driven men and women are now preparing themselves for their next life achievements. We help them build a blueprint for their next meaningful journey.

Through the First Responder Retirement Academy, we help America's retiring first responders discover a new mission and purpose for their lives. They get a blueprint to build their next active 30 years. They find they are happier and more content because they have meaning and purpose for each day. They can contribute again, which is who they really are internally. They plan their next personal legacy.

The following testimonial from a 30-year veteran woman police officer told us that she began to successfully find her next mission and purpose:

> *"Susan, I just can't tell you how much I enjoyed the retirement class that you and Jim presented. It truly relieved much of my anxiety and gave me a road map to success in my future pursuits after this stage of my working life. Facing the challenges of retirement from law enforcement head-on with all the pathways that you both brought to the forefront gave me a newfound confidence in jumping into the next stage of my life. Before the class, I was so stressed out about retirement, that I wasn't feeling good about the end of this juncture. At 58 years old, I knew I couldn't continue this way like a [spring chicken]. I was afraid to pull the plug. As we get older, we just have to face the*

music that we are not in our 20s anymore. To remind myself of this very fact, I just had to laugh about being the oldest woman out on patrol as I start to feel new aches and pains....Thank you both so very much!"

Conclusion: Don't Try This At Home...Alone

We were lost on how to build a successful, let alone a nationwide, business until we signed on with the Retirement Coaches Association learning program. We first tried to build a new business at home and alone. For years, we just could not get any real traction until we started looking outside the four walls of our home.

The Retirement Coached Association education and mentoring program has made a significant and positive impact on our lives and, ultimately, the lives of retiring first responders and their families. The variety of topics, online live teaching platform, and individual coaching meetings are well done and applicable. They gave us a clear and detailed entrepreneurial map to building a successful business and healthy lifestyle. Thank you, RCA!

To learn more about the First Responder Retirement Academy visit www.FirstResponderRetirement.com. Follow us on Facebook at www.facebook.com/events/338356163737620/ and on LinkedIn at www.linkedin.com/in/jim-hyde-66b6a32a/. Contact us via email at info@FirstResponderRetirement.com or by calling 916-895-1536.

References

1. Kets de Vries, M. (2014). "Managing People: The Dark Side of Retirement." *Harvard Business Review*, 2014. Cambridge, Mass., Harvard University.

Nurses In Action In Retirement
By Andrea R Jennings

Introduction

Retirement at last! It sounds exciting and it is something we all look forward to achieving one day. Over a period of time, I have attended countless retirement celebrations for nurses and have asked the question "What is your plan for retirement?" In most instances, the response is vague and not comprehensive. It is clear that contemplation about the concept of retirement is needed by each individual. Facilitating deeper thoughts about retirement has been my calling for decades, as I have had countless conversations with nurses on the topic. It brings me great joy as a certified professional retirement coach to engage nurses as they develop, implement, and evaluate their plan for retirement. "Retirement at last and I have a plan," are the words I hope to hear!

Nursing is a dynamic profession that is full of opportunities throughout one's career. As nurses, we spend our time caring for others, critically thinking, problem-solving, inventing, teaching, collaborating, and communicating effectively with entities within society. When retirement comes upon us, we soon realize we have become very efficient in the skills aforementioned and these same skills will serve us well in anything we would like to pursue in retirement. Recognizing that we have such an amazing set of skills can enable us to establish a second career, become activists, volunteer at organizations, or become entrepreneurs in our retirement years. Retirement opportunities are surely plentiful for the retired nurse.

A Nurse's Journey

As nurses, our careers are long lasting, we probably all started off on a medical surgical unit and then set our sights on a specialty area whether it was pediatrics, intensive care, emergency department, hospice, education, ambulatory care, or case management just to name a few. As we progressed in our careers, some of us pursued a higher degree whether it was obtaining a BSN, MSN, DNP, or PhD. In addition to nursing degrees, some of us went out of our comfort zone and pursued degrees in other disciplines. Obtaining certifications and certificates in many areas of nursing is quite a common practice for all of us to do as we progress through our careers. It is absolutely amazing how we are afforded with such diverse opportunities and experiences throughout our careers. In addition to all our degrees, certifications, and work experiences, some of us donate our time to address the ongoing health issues in our communities. Others spend countless hours educating and advocating on behalf of friends and family on how to manage health issues. As nurses, we have many passions that manifest in both work and non-work settings.

Being a nurse is a journey that lasts a lifetime from the beginning of reciting the Florence Nightingale Pledge at our graduation pinning ceremonies to the culmination where we say that we are a "retired" nurse. As you move towards retirement or if you are in retirement, it may be worthwhile to revisit the pledge and reflect accordingly. Here is the Nightingale Pledge:

"I solemnly pledge myself before God and in the presence of this assembly to pass my life in purity and to practice my profession faithfully. I will abstain from whatever is deleterious and mischievous, and shall not take or knowingly administer any harmful drug. I shall do all in my power to maintain and elevate the standard of my profession and will hold in confidence all personal matters committed to my keeping and all family affairs coming to my knowledge in the practice of my calling. I shall be loyal to my work and devoted towards the welfare of those committed to my care."[1]

Personal Reflection

Upon personal reflection, I often find myself comparing nursing to a colorful rainbow. There is an array of colors in a rainbow symbolizing the many beautiful opportunities that are presented to nurses. These opportunities bring great joy to nurses as they care and share their talents with individuals, groups, and communities. A rainbow symbolizes hope and from a folklorist viewpoint there is said to be a pot of gold at the end. Our pot of gold is knowing that we positively impacted a countless number of patients in need over the span of our careers. In reality, there is no end to a rainbow, just as we know as nurses we often want to continue to give the best of ourselves in some manner in retirement and there are endless possibilities.

Three-Step Nurse Action Retirement Exercise

As a certified retirement coach, I have coached nurses nearing retirement and there is a three-step Nurse Action Retirement Exercise that I devised that will assist nurses as they entertain retirement or if they are already in retirement. Step one is to make a list of nursing-related activities they would want to participate in during retirement, and designate whether they would want to do them on a full- or part-time basis. They then construct another list of non-nursing-related activities that they would want to experience in retirement and again determine if they will be full- or part-time ventures.

Step one is needed in order to pinpoint activities you would enjoy doing in retirement whether they are nursing or non-nursing related. Making lists will allow you to thoroughly explore the activities you identified. Next, you should think about any barriers (i.e., financial, time constraints, social, relationship, emotional, and knowledge) that may be preventing you from participating in the activities you identified on your lists. Think about how you will overcome these barriers and come to terms on how realistically you can move forward with each activity. If there are a lot of activities listed, you may want to rank them in order of importance based on how likely you are going to engage in this activity. Focus on your top three activities in each category and write them down.

In step two, identifying your strengths and weaknesses with regards to your ability to participate in each top activity is recommended. The following two questions need to be answered: How will your professional and personal strengths aid you in your ability to engage in your selected activities? How will your professional and personal weaknesses delay you from pursuing your activities?

This step is important because you realistically need to consider your strengths and weaknesses both professionally and personally to determine your success with the activity. After answering these questions and upon reflection in this step, you may want to re-evaluate your top activities based on your responses to the above questions. It is common to move activities around and decide on new top activities.

Step three places an emphasis on action with the top three nursing-related activities and with the top three non-nursing-related activities. After reviewing your responses for steps one and two from up above, you should develop a broad goal and then determine the tasks needed to help you achieve this goal. Identifying resources to help you achieve your goals is recommended in this phase. You should at this point write down time frames in which you will start engaging in each activity.

Case Study

Let us see how I would apply these steps in retirement coaching for a nurse approaching retirement in the following hypothetical case study:

Nurse X has been a nurse for 35 years and is currently a nurse manager in an emergency department in a large health care system. She is 63 years old and will retire in three months. She is single and has three children, along with four grandchildren. She has had to deal with her share of politics and has managed the Emergency Department (ED) for the last 20 years. She is looking forward to her retirement but labels this retirement as a "semi-retirement."

The three-step process was utilized in our retirement coaching sessions. In step one, Nurse X compiled her list of nursing related activities and non-nursing related activities. Amazingly, she had 15 items in each category, and I began to realize what she meant by a "semi-retirement." After a few coaching sessions, Nurse X was able to prioritize the top three activities in each group. She decided not to list spending time with family because she already makes that a priority in her life now. The top three in her non-nursing-related activity list were:

1.   Volunteering at an animal shelter.

2. Becoming a climate change activist
3. Volunteering to help children read.

The top three on her nursing-related activity list included:

1. Becoming politically active in advocating safety for nurses in the ED.
2. Becoming certified in meditation.
3. Mentoring nursing students.

We discussed the barriers that might be in place for the activities that Nurse X listed. With the non-nursing-related activities, a knowledge barrier was identified with how to become a climate-change activist as Nurse X did not know where to start. No barriers were identified for the other two activities. For the nursing-related activities, a knowledge deficit for the meditation activity was identified because Nurse X did not know where she could get training. She also identified finances as a potential barrier for this activity due to the costs of the meditation training.

Nurse X was ready to move to step two and identified professional weaknesses with regards to becoming politically active, becoming a political climate-change activist, and learning meditation. In her professional career, she never really had time to pursue political activities and her political competency is in question. She doesn't know what skills are needed to become a successful climate-change activist. Nurse X never incorporated meditation in her daily life and so this is a new activity that will require learning new skills and knowledge.

Her professional strengths include being familiar with issues that impact nurses in the ED and these experiences will allow her to be a strong advocate for political change. Her previous experiences as a mentor for new nurses in the ED department will serve her well in future nurse mentoring activities.

In terms of her personal strengths, she is an avid reader and worked in pediatrics prior to management, therefore she is well suited to help children with their reading. Nurse X has had a variety of pets throughout the years and is comfortable with caring for pets. She did not list any personal weaknesses with regard to the activities she selected. Based on her responses in step two, Nurse X decided to keep all her activities that she listed and did not alter her list.

Step three was the final step that we discussed, and it is here where Nurse X formulated personal goals for each of her activities, listed tasks that were needed to complete her goal, identified resources to help move her forward, and considered time frames.

Non-Nursing-Related Activities

1. **Volunteering at an animal shelter (part time)**

   Goal: To be aware of what is expected when volunteering at an animal shelter.

Tasks: Locate a job description that highlights volunteering at an animal shelter. Contact the manager of an animal shelter to talk about volunteer opportunities.

Resources: Local animal shelters, Humane Society, Pet Smart Volunteers, PAWS, and Animal Protective League.

Time Frame: One month from now.

2. **Becoming a climate-change activist (part time)**

   Goal: To become knowledgeable about becoming a climate-change activist.

   Tasks: Read articles about climate change to determine specific interests.

   Resources: Local Sierra Club, 350.org, and Citizens' Climate Lobby.

   Time Frame: Two months from now.

3. **Volunteering to help children read (part time)**

   Goal: To become cognizant of the different learning environments in which kids can be taught to read.

   Tasks: Identify teaching resources that focus on helping kids to read.

Resources: Target the local libraries, AARP Foundation Experience Corps, and Oasis Institute.

Time Frame: One month from now.

Nursing related activities:

1. **Becoming politically active in advocating safety for nurses in the ED (part time)**

   Goal: To determine what it means to become politically active.

   Tasks: Purchase a health policy book geared toward nurses who are active in the political arena.

   Resources: American Nurses Association and Emergency Nurses Association websites.

   Time Frame: Three months from now

2. **Becoming certified in meditation (part time)**

   Goal: To research the significance of being certified in meditation.

   Tasks: Locate resources on the internet that describe the different types of meditation.

   Resources: Local hospitals, private trainers, The Veda Center, and Spirit Rock Meditation Center.

Time Frame: Two months from now.

3. **Mentoring nursing students (part time)**

Goal: To determine the types of learning environments in which I can become a mentor for nursing students.

Tasks: Identify resources that may help nursing students.

Resources: Local community colleges and universities that offer a nursing degree, Mentorship Nursing CE Course, Academy of Medical Surgical Nurses (AMSN) Mentoring Program.

Time Frame: One month from now.

Certainly, there are many other strategies that are used in retirement coaching, but these first steps will serve as a blueprint for any retirement plan. Over time, the goals, tasks, resources, and time frames may need to be revised as this plan is a work in progress. Working through the Nurse Action Retirement Exercise with Nurse X took several sessions and illustrates the need for the ongoing support from a retirement coach.

Three-Step Nurse Action Retirement Exercise Practice Sheet

Step 1

- List all nursing-related retirement activities (specify full time, part time, and barriers).

- List all non-nursing-related retirement activities (specify full time, part time, and barriers).
- Circle your top three activities in each category

Step 2

Nursing-related activities

1. _____

2. _____

3. _____

Non-nursing-related activities

1. _____

2. _____

3. _____

- Write down personal strengths/weaknesses for each activity.
- Write down professional strengths/weaknesses for each activity.
- Note any changes with your activities here:

_____

_____

_____

_____

Step 3

Nursing-related activities (list goal, tasks, resources, and time frame for each activity)

1. _____

2. _____

3. _____

Non-nursing-related activities (list goal, tasks, resources, and time frame for each activity)

1. _____

2. _____

3. _____

Conclusion

As nurses approach retirement and for those who are already retired, we all have a story to tell about our experiences as a nurse. All our unique experiences will lead us down different paths into retirement. I have extreme gratitude for all the nurses who have come before me. Retirement can bring on feelings of exhilaration, pride, and joy, but after a while one may feel disconnected and disengaged. Eventually, some soul searching will have to occur in figuring out what your goals are in retirement. The guidance from a retirement coach can be very enlightening before retirement and during retirement. My clients have cited the following benefits of having a retirement coach:

- "Discovering my goals in retirement with my coach as a facilitator was truly eye opening and the sessions allowed me to get my life on track."
- "My sessions with my retirement coach allowed me to do deep soul searching".
- "My retirement coach guided me in my reflections on what I wanted to do in my retirement years."

As nurses, we know the value of life and so we should live it to the fullest even in our retirement years.

About The Author

Andrea Jennings is a Certified Professional Retirement Coach (CPRC) and has been a nurse for over 30 years. She has worked extensively in nursing research, community health, gerontology case management, pediatrics, and orthopedics. She has been in academia for over twenty-five years and has taught at all levels in nursing. She has a doctorate degree in Public Health, master's degrees in Nursing and Education, and a bachelor's degree in Nursing. She has dedicated this chapter to her son, Thomas, who is in the Marine Corps Boot Camp. He has inspired her to move forward with her goals in the next chapter of her life. Contact Andrea at ActionRetirement@gmail.com

References

1. Anna Caroline Maxwell and Amy Elizabeth Pope, "The Florence Nightingale Pledge," *Practical Nursing: A Textbook for Nurses and a Handbook for All who Care for the Sick*, New York: Putnam, 1910.

Charting A New Course After
The Sale Of Your Business
By Sherry Dutra

"Wait! I can't do this. I'm not ready!" Are these the words of a patient about to get a root canal? Perhaps this is coming from a first-time roller coaster rider – just as they get strapped in. Or, maybe a child shouts these words as they hesitate to jump in the water to test their new swimming skills. All might be possibilities. The truth is they are the words of many a retiring business owner who is about to sell the business in which they have invested their heart and soul. Will this happen to you or someone you love?

The Need For Personal Transition Planning

Why would a highly successful business owner need help with their personal transition into retirement? Because it is not as easy as it looks. Time and time again, I hear stories of business owners who are practically at the finish line of selling their business and suddenly they call a halt to the process. As you might imagine, this is happening after much of the work of putting the transaction into place has already occurred, wasting significant time, money, and opportunity. Ideally, at least five years before the target date for the sale of the business, owners should be starting to plan for the personal transition associated with this momentous event. Investing the time and energy to plan increases the likelihood that you are ready

137

when your business is ready, and increases the joy and fulfillment of post-ownership life. Joan* was co-owner of a mid-sized retail establishment. As she and her partner considered selling the business, she oscillated between saying it was not time to sell and entertaining notions of how much any new owner would need her to stay around for a year or two after a sale. Joan was completely burned out yet her identity was so wrapped up in the business, she could not see herself without it. She simply did not know who she would be in retirement. This was not only impacting her work life and health, but also created strain in the relationship with her co-owner, who happened to be her husband.

Preparing For The Sale

When smart business owners start thinking about selling their business, they typically assemble a team to support them. That team might include a CPA, an investment banker, an estate attorney, a business valuation professional, and a financial planner, to name a few. Creating a team to assist with navigating the myriad complexities involved from pre-sale to post-sale is sound business sense.

Yet, there is a critical team member who is usually missing from the equation. That team member is the professional who helps the business owner with the personal transition they will face.

When the time comes that you start seriously considering the sale of your business or its transfer to family members, what this process will mean to you on a personal level is usually the last thing on your mind. It may be pushed to the back burner or not even identified as a critical part of the process. Time, effort, and money are poured into other crucial aspects of preparing for the sale. Rightly so, you are focusing on whether the right conditions are in place to optimize the value of your business. Is your industry growing or contracting? What is the current state of the business itself? Do you have strong processes in place, a solid management team, and business practices that allow for the smooth operation of the business?

You have worked with the transition team to evaluate your business, you have corrected any identified deficiencies, and now you are attracting potential buyers. This is exciting, is it not? Absolutely! Up to this point, you may even have been looking forward to wrapping things up and embarking on the next phase of your journey. Yet, often, this is now the time that what this transition means to you on a personal basis rears its ugly head if you have not planned, in advance. Anxiety may begin to build as you face the reality that you are about to experience an enormous change in your life. You may even get all the way to the meeting in which you will sign the paperwork when you suddenly panic and step on the brakes. This is unfortunate and it is avoidable.

Equally important to preparing the business and choosing the right time to sell is preparing yourself. Selling your business is a major life transition. Like any significant transition, leaping into the unknown without a plan can feel like practicing high-flying acrobatics with no safety net. Too often, many soon-to-be retirees never get beyond a vague sense of what life will be like after selling their business.

During the first year or two after a sale, many business owners report feeling lost and spend their time trying to figure out what to do with themselves. While they may have more money and free time than ever before, they suffer in silence and are unsure of what to do or who to turn to for help. So, they retreat, second-guess their decision to sell the business, and think about all they are missing from the old days.

The thoughts they had of playing golf five days a week or vacationing in various parts of the world are not as satisfying as anticipated, nor do they come close to filling their days with personally meaningful endeavors. When the glow of an extended vacation wears off, stark reality can set in, prompting the question of "now what?"

A Holistic View

What constitutes a holistic view of life after the sale? Of course, financial considerations are an important component. However, it is a myth to believe that having your finances under control, as the only preparation, will allow this phase of life to smoothly unfold. A holistic view takes into consideration the spiritual, mental/emotional, physical, and social aspects, as well. Attending to each of these areas, in addition to your finances, sets the stage for you to be ready when your business is ready. Consequently, you will be far less likely to pull the plug at the last minute or sink into anxiety or depression after the sale. Let us look at each of these additional areas, beyond your finances, and explore the first small steps toward creating your personal transition plan.

Spiritual

The word "spiritual" means different things to different people, and there seems to be no clear consensus on the definition. For the purposes of the discussion here, spirituality is defined as the core values that guide how you live your life. They are the principles that drive you and what you hold as most important to you.

Examining your values from time to time helps to ensure that you not only stay aligned with your authentic self, but also choose values that truly represent how you want to live your life. You see, values can also be a product of your exposure to your family, your community, and so on. You may unconsciously take on the values of others simply by being taught, over the course of your life, what you should want. Choose those that resonate the most with who you are and then take the time to articulate them and clearly define what they mean uniquely to you.

When your values are being honored, you feel a sense of peace and happiness. When they are not, discontent sets in. In terms of retirement, in order to plan a post-sale life that is in alignment with what drives you, it stands to reason that you must gain clarity on what those values are and what they mean to you.

Values Exercise

What are the values that drive you? Take a moment to identify your top 5 values – those that you cannot live without. Then, write down a few words or phrases that define what each value means to you. Here are some sample values to get you started.

Abundance	Accomplishment
Adventure	Balance
Beauty	Boldness
Calmness	Clarity
Commitment	Community
Compassion	Connection
Contribution	Creativity

Dependability	Determination
Discipline	Enjoyment
Enthusiasm	Excellence
Faith	Family
Fitness	Freedom
Fun	Generosity
Health	Honesty
Humor	Independence
Integrity	Inquisitiveness
Joy	Leadership
Love	Loyalty
Making a Difference	Openness
Orderliness	Personal Growth
Positivity	Practicality
Recognition	Results-oriented
Self-reliance	Service
Structure	Teamwork
Vision	Vitality

Top 5 Values Defined:

1. _____
2. _____
3. _____
4. _____
5. _____

As you consider the values you have identified and defined, how might they begin to inform you of what needs to be a part of your post-sale life? What are your initial ideas about how these values will be honored in new ways?

Mental/Emotional

The role that a business owner's mindset plays in retirement is understated at best. Often, their feelings and ideas of what retirement will be like are a far cry from what reality will bring. In many cases, post-sale life does not unfold as expected which leads to a time of grief and regret over their decision to sell in the first place. Addressing the mental and emotional aspects of retirement contributes significantly to your overall wellness.

As a business owner, you most likely have a passion for the service or product that you offer and have been driven toward providing value while growing and sustaining your business over the years. Now, you need a new outlet for that passion. Too often, we conflate what we *do* with who we *are*.

It is no wonder then, that losing one's sense of identity is one of the top issues faced in retirement.

We all need purpose, meaning, and joy in our lives. Endless days of freedom from responsibility and time commitments may feel enticing at first. Yet, it does not take long for having no reason to get up in the morning to deflate that initial balloon of happiness and leave you at loose ends.

John* had been the founder and CEO of a successful consulting practice for over 25 years. Guiding the practice through several economic ups and downs, John was proud of his firm's reputation, the team he had mentored and grown, and the contributions of time and money that had been made to better the local community. At 60, he wanted to move to the next phase of his life. Working with a team of advisors, John readied the business for sale. Unfortunately, John was heavily focused on the business and had given little consideration to how he would spend his days after the business sold. Within a few months after the sale, he was feeling completely at loose ends and saying "yes" to every request that came along to be on a board. John did not know who he was if he was not the owner of a business and was grasping at anything that could potentially fill the void.

Replacing one's work identity is not accomplished in an afternoon. It requires investing the time to step back, early in the process of readying your business for sale, to reflect on this question. Who do I want to become? Remember that you still have much to offer the world. What might be something you have always wanted to do, but have never found the time or the courage to try? What are your core strengths and competencies that you truly enjoy using?

As you move through this exploration, involve others who know you well, especially friends and family. From their perspective, what ideas do they have to contribute regarding what might be next for you? Asking for the input of others aids in broadening your view and sparking greater insight to fuel your own introspection.

Clarity on who you want to become, then leads to exploring what do you want to do to express that. Does your next stage include some form of work? If so, what does that look like? Is it working for someone else, consulting, or perhaps starting another business? Is it a part-time or full-time pursuit? Or, are you leaning toward a time of connecting with family, involvement with your community and/or engaging in new hobbies or other fun activities? Are you envisioning some combination of the above?

When the time comes that you sell and make the transition, keep in mind that it will still take time to adjust even when you have a plan in place. The difference will be that, with a comprehensive and well-thought out plan, your adjustment will be much smoother. Think about any other major change in your life, such as when you moved out on your own for the first time, when you married or shared a home with someone, or when you had your first child. Typically, these are all major transitions that you likely planned for. Did you immediately adjust to these new stages of life or did it take a period of getting acclimated? Most would agree that a time of adjustment was involved in every transition. Likely, too, these were not passive experiences, but times in which you had to take action to make each of these stages work for you. Your retirement transition is no different.

Physical

Addressing your physical health is another key element to your overall well-being in retirement. What role do proper nutrition, exercise, sleep, and relaxation currently play in your life? For many business owners, operating the business can become all-consuming and good intentions fall by the wayside. Do not beat yourself up if you have some work to do in this area. Be honest with yourself on your current state of physical health and select one area to begin making improvements. The sooner you start, the greater the benefits, and the easier it will be to maintain a healthy lifestyle in retirement. Oftentimes people will say that when they retire, they will start exercising, stop eating fast food, get more sleep, and so on, because they will have more time to attend to their physical health. Unfortunately, habits can be difficult to break and the longer you wait to do so, the more challenging it will be. More time on your hands in retirement, may end up meaning more time staying sedentary because that is what your habit has been. Consequently, I encourage you to continue the positive health habits you already have in place and to make a commitment to expand into any elements you are missing. By the time you are ready to sell your business and retire, you will have strong habits to support your physical well-being during your retirement years. Even if you are already experiencing some type of ailment, taking steps to do as much as you are capable of will support your ability to thrive.

- **Nutrition:** How well are you currently eating? Do you find that due to the demands of your work that you too often find yourself eating fast food or skipping meals? How can you make healthy choices on a more regular basis? Healthy choices include things like colorful fruits and vegetables, whole grains, lean cuts of meat, skinless poultry, fish, beans and eggs, and foods with less added sugar. Talk with your doctor to find out what is right for you.

- **Exercise:** Do you already have a regular workout or exercise routine in place, or do you struggle to find the time or motivation to incorporate a fitness regimen? Pick something you like to do and get out and do it. Perhaps you loved to ride a bike when you were a child, or you enjoy a brisk walk. Are you interested in strength training and want to start lifting weights? Find something that appeals to you and get your body moving. As with nutrition, be sure that you check with your doctor before starting an exercise regimen.

- **Sleep:** There seems to be a general consensus that between seven and eight hours of sleep per night is an optimal target to aspire to. How many hours of sleep are you currently averaging per night? How rested do you feel when you wake up? Most fitness trackers today allow you to track your sleep so this can give you a baseline to start with. If you are having difficulty sleeping, pay attention to what you are doing close to bedtime. Using screens, eating late, or exercising too close to bedtime can all impact your sleep. Meditation is a tool that can improve the quality of sleep as well. Of course, if you consistently are having difficulty with sleep, there may be something else in play that requires medical attention.

- **Relaxation:** Are you ever off the clock? Can you allow yourself some time that is not associated with being productive? Does relaxation for you involve an activity of some sort, like golf or playing with your grandchildren? Is relaxation sitting outdoors reading a book? What is relaxing for you? While you are still working, it might be as simple as giving yourself a few moments each hour to take three deep breaths. In retirement, what will be the leisure activities that you would like to incorporate into your week? What types of things have you always been curious about? Perhaps you always wanted to learn how to paint landscapes, play an instrument, explore your genealogy, or learn to dance. It does not matter what it is. Begin considering those activities or interests that will spark your desire to stay involved. Where are you already doing well in the physical arena? Where might you need to make improvements? What one change are you willing to commit to as you begin addressing your physical well-being right now?

Social

Many of you may already have a strong social network around you. Over the years of owning your business, you likely have connections throughout the business community, charitable organizations, employees, clients, and customers. On an average day, you may interact with dozens of people. After retirement, this daily interaction may be significantly less which feeds a sense of isolation over time. Currently, how much time do you spend around others each week? What will replace that social connectivity after you sell?

Different people have varying needs when it comes to interaction with others. Yet, whether you are an extrovert or an introvert, as humans, we all need connection. It does not matter if you have 100 people that you consider good friends or prefer to have a close-knit group of ten. What is important is having a network of social relationships that will continue beyond the sale of your business.

As you approach retirement, developing relationships beyond the world of work takes intention. You might be thinking, *"If I'm still busy with my business, how can I possibly make time to expand my network?"* People make time for what is important to them. Consequently, if you embrace the value that relationships and a sense of belonging contribute to your overall wellness, you will find the time.

The quality of your relationships is a factor as well. Who are you building relationships with? Jim Rohn, motivational speaker, has said, "You are the average of the five people you spend the most time with." Ensure that you are surrounding yourself with generally positive people who are supportive and lift one another up. This does not mean that you should avoid a relationship with someone who occasionally has a bad day. We are human and that is completely natural. Spending time around those with a consistent negative attitude and who regularly drain your energy is where you would exercise caution. Pay attention to your own outlook, as well. You do not want to become the person that others choose to avoid.

As you begin to explore the social arena of your retirement, here are some questions to consider.

- How might you continue some of your work-related connections after retirement?
- What groups are you interested in and could start to explore before you sell?
- What relationships with extended family might you cultivate?
- What shared interests do you have with neighbors or others in the community?

Conclusion

There are many moving parts to retirement and it constitutes a significant transition in your life. That transition into the next stage of your life can be an amazing time or it can be fraught with disenchantment. You get to choose how it turns out for you. When you pull together the team that will help you prepare for the sale, include an objective professional such as a retirement coach to support you in crafting your future.

Each person's transition to post-sale life is unique and there is not one answer that will work for everyone. There can be a wide variety of possibilities for you that will allow your retirement years to unfold with joy and fulfillment. Give yourself the gift of time to explore and shape that next phase of your life. Doing so will significantly reduce the stress involved when the right buyer emerges. Investing in yourself by preparing for your own personal transition is every bit as important as preparing for the actual sale of your business. Preparing early will allow you to seamlessly move from pre-sale to post-sale with the confidence that you know what you are retiring to. You have worked hard to create the business you have today. That did not happen without planning. Your post-sale life calls for an equal amount of preparation.

About the Author

Sherry Dutra is an executive, career, and retirement coach and facilitator who works with corporate leaders and business owners in small to mid-size businesses, across the span of their careers. She helps them to accelerate business outcomes and team performance, navigate their own career path, and transition to retirement with ease using proven methodologies and strategies that get results. She is recognized as a Professional Certified Coach by the International Coach Federation and holds multiple coaching certifications including a Certified Professional Retirement Coach designation. If you would like to uncover and address hidden challenges that may be sabotaging your success, leverage your strengths, and accelerate your progress toward the results you desire, contact Sherry@DutraAssociates.com for a complimentary consultation or go to DutraAssociates.com to register for her monthly newsletter and receive free Career Continuum Wheels to help you hone in on what is most important no matter the stage of your career.

* Name and specifics have been changed to protect confidentiality.

Life After Caregiving
By Carmel Murphy-Kotyan

Caregiving

A quote from the former First Lady Rosalyn Carter, founder of the Rosalyn Carter Institute for Caregiving, says, "Caregiving is hard work...it is important that we listen to caregivers in order to know what their needs are and then address the specific needs they identify." Having our community understand and acknowledge our caregiving role is necessary, but unfortunately the struggles and stresses of caring for our aging loved ones are not always recognized. Caregiving is hard. Harder than you ever imagined. As the primary family caregiver, you have gone through the many stages of care. As a certified caregiver consultant through The Caregiving Years, I have been trained in understanding the six meaningful stages of the caregiving journey.

Stage 1, The Expectant Caregiver: Planning for the journey ahead.

Stage 2, The Freshman Caregiver: Recognizing your caree's needs and stepping in to help.

Stage 3, The Entrenched Caregiver: Being in the trenches. The most stressful, overwhelming, and exhausting stage.

Stage 4, The Pragmatic Caregiver: Having a system in place. You know what to do.

Stage 5, The Transitioning Caregiver: Letting go.

Stage 6, The Goodspeed Caregiver: Beginning again.

In this chapter, I am going to focus on the last two stages: the **Transitioning Caregiver**, who is at the stage of letting go of one's role, and the final stage, called the **Goodspeed Caregiver**, where your loved one has passed and you must take the step forward to begin your life after caregiving.

There are 40 million unpaid caregivers in the United States today, caring for older adults, aging parents, or spouses. The average caregiver is a middle-aged female. Many are considered "sandwich generational," in that they care for both their children and their parents. Fifty-six percent work full time. Common help that family caregivers provide is medical, emotional, financial, and domestic (running errands and household chores). Common struggles are stress, overwhelm, loneliness, and resentment. Letting go of your guilt, fears, and resentments will help you grow and get ready to begin again, building on your values, gifts, passions, and purpose.

Letting Go

Through our own aging and growth process, a time will come when you will recognize that it is time to let go. Let go of your frustrations, anger, and ego. Let go of your assumptions, regrets, and fears.

Accepting the reality that you are in and embracing it.

When your aging parent/spouse is at the end of their life, the time is ripe to breathe, settle, hold their hand, and recount some happy memories. They have been through so much in their final years, health care systems, surgeries, pain, and loss. The days of fixing are at an end. It is now time to let go of doing and just be – be there, listen, laugh, and reminisce. Accept the reality. Your loved one is now in their final weeks/months in this life, and wants to spend it with their loved ones, in the space you would have discussed earlier in your caregiving journey. End-of-life planning is an important part of your role as a caregiver. Think about their legacy. What is it they will want to be remembered for? While keeping them safe and pain free is important, multiple hospital trips, testing, and surgeries are not what anyone wants in their now limited time of life. Hiring a hospice or a professional caregiver will help provide the comfort care they need. But you are their primary caregiver. You know them best. Embrace that. Be there with them.

This stage of caregiving, called the Transitioning stage, is emotionally consuming, because it is about both your caree and you. While your caree is transitioning out of this life, you are transitioning out of your role as a caregiver. As you spend your time with your caree, you now need to think about your own transition that is ahead of you. The first step is always awareness; recognizing your life is going to change also. What will that look like? The second step is letting go. You have absorbed many hard emotions during your caregiving journey and now you need to ask yourself what it is that you need to let go of before you consider your next step?

Let go of guilt: You have done the best work under the circumstances, your time constraints, and with the knowledge that you had. Feeling grief and regrets for your loved one is understandable. But living with guilt and self-criticism will cripple your life. There are lots of stumbles in caregiving; we learn from them and move on. Doing your best work is a value to live by but that does not equate with perfectionism. Our best work is the best work we can do with the knowledge, resources, restraints, and finances we have at that time. You have loved your caree and have done your best work. Now let go of the guilt and concentrate on your life ahead.

Let go of grudges and resentment: When caregiving starts, it is common to have conversations with family and friends about the needs ahead for your loved one. It is common that many will say that they will be there to help. It is common that many will not. So often, the care for a loved one falls on one or two family members. It can illicit anger, resentment, and grudges. Let go of these feelings. You only have control over your own reactions and responses to a situation. Why those family members did not persevere in helping and supporting you is no longer relevant. Realize that their noncommitment has to do with their own issues and fears. It will be of value to you not to take it personally; to let it go. We each live with the decisions we make in life. Not getting the help and support that you had hoped for can be extremely frustrating. You can find a hundred reasons why is it unfair, how they could have helped, and why it added to your stress and overwhelm. While these thoughts may be validated, it will not help to hold on to them. Forgiving transitions you from past to present. They chose their decisions; now you choose yours for your personal well-being and knowledge of self-worth.

Let go of fear: Our natural state of being is to remain in our comfort zone, where we feel safe, have a set routine, and know what is ahead of us. This is good; it is free of risk, stress, and anxiety. However, stepping outside our comfort zone will benefit our self-growth, curiosity, and courage – and this is so worth it. We have only one life to live and it is a journey. And in my opinion, it is a labyrinth journey, in that we learn and grow in different stages and sometimes must fall back to see the true picture. What we did not see in our past experiences, is now obvious to us as our growth deepens. To mature and grow requires that we push past our vulnerability, we take risks, and we are ready to fail. None of this is easy but what you will gain will add peace and contentment to your life. And that is what we all strive for. When you fail to some degree at this step into bravery, and you will fail at some point, see that failure as a teacher – and grow from it. Know that your comfort zone shrinks as we get older, so the time is now to step outside it.

To take that first step outside your comfort zone starts with awareness – awareness of what your fears are and why, and understanding of the benefits when you try to step forward. Your first step may be having that difficult conversation that you have been avoiding, trying something that you have been curious about for some time, or moving to a new area, career, or relationship. With a racing heart, you will take a baby step and you will gain the resilience and strength that you crave. Life invites you to live in a growth zone – go ahead, take your first step.

Here are some questions to ask yourself:

- What changes must you accomplish so that you are free to do what you most want to do with our life?
- What are the obstacles that you see as prohibiting you from taking the next step to live your best life?
- What do you need to liberate yourself from?

Beginning Again

When your role as a caregiver ends, you may feel suspended in space. Your life as a caregiver was limited and small, now it may seem vast and empty. The loss of your caree, your role, and your purpose has been taken from you. It can take time to settle into your new reality and overcome the grief you may be feeling – two months or two years – and investigating a process or routine that will help you recognize your self-worth and curiosity to what lies ahead is a beginning. Listening to your friends' and family's advice without comment, allowing yourself time to sit with it, and acknowledging your self-worth will help you make these decisions, and vice versa. Decluttering, meditation, prayer, and continuing to let go, will open the pathway ahead for you.

This stage of caregiving is called the Goodspeed Caregiver and relies on ruminating on and journaling what your values, gifts, passions, and purpose are. This will be your vehicle.

Values: Googling a list of values is easy, but think deeply before you choose yours. Write them down because these values are ones that you will practice and live by. Stick them on your bathroom mirror or put them on an app on your phone, so that you can review them every day. Do you want to remain curious, to be a lifelong learner? This will help find your new purpose. Do you want to control your reactions and responses to circumstance? This will help your relationships and help you live in peace. Do you want to embrace trust? This may be a spiritual thing or just trust in yourself, and will help in overcoming fears. What are your values? I can think of nothing more crucial to a happy life than identifying and aligning your values to how you live.

Gifts: We have all been blessed with gifts. Recognizing, appreciating, and using these natural gifts is important. You have learned so much on your caregiving journey. You have gained unique skills, talents, and wisdom. You now have a lot to give back to your family and community. How will you use these gifts?

Passion: As kids, our passions came naturally. We recognized our interests and went after them – baseball, art, skateboarding, etc. As adults, we do not prioritize our passions because of our workload, commitments, and distractions. But why not? Those passions that bubble within us should be given status. They are part of our authentic selves. And I believe our life's journey is about fulfilling our inner being or true selves. Because you are starting a new episode of your life and taking on a new role, let that role include your passions. What have you been curious about that may still be buried inside you? Try it again. The new technology and opportunities that now exist will help you master this step forward. Prioritizing your passion may mean letting go of other things. Taking that class that you have an interest in may mean not having the time to make dinner that evening. That is okay.

Reconnecting and prioritizing your authentic self will change your life in ways that you had forgotten even existed. Letting go of ego – of what others think of you – and opening your heart to who you really are will bring an abundance of joy to your life. The wisdom you have gained through caregiving will help you understand how fleeting a life can be. You are at an age now to live that life. You are ready.

Purpose: Living a passive lifestyle without purpose is much too common in this world. We wade through our daily routines and our distractions, and are content in our comfort zone. We live and die in this small world that we have made for ourselves. However, I believe, that there are two types of purposes that we need to embrace. One is **Doing** what we have a curiosity about based on our values, gifts, and passions. Doing the activity, travel, or volunteering that brings meaning to your life is important. You may have learned a lot about this, having read the other chapters of this book, so I am not going to delve into that. I am going to discuss the second part of our purpose, which is the **Being**. Being is derived from self-growth.

Going through the COVID-19 pandemic of being quarantined has caused a lot of isolation and loneliness for many people. And while I certainly understand the anguish that this has caused and have done many presentations on this topic, I also have learned that there are values to alone time – some exquisite values. The stillness of alone time brings healing to your mind and soul. It will provide time to knit and heal. In this stillness, you will return to your authentic self. Too many of us go through our lives without ever meeting ourselves. Take the time to investigate. Meeting and living with your true self will be the most life-changing work you will ever do. Go ahead. Sit in stillness.

As kids, we live in the moment. We prioritize our being – playing, eating, giggling – while our doing is secondary.

As adults, our life gets reversed. We prioritize our doing – our busyness, multitasking, and chores – while our being is barely remembered.

As elders we tend to fall back into just being – sitting, watching, and thinking – while our doing is considered by many as incapacitated.

As adults, pushing ourselves to balance our life will help you grow. That is what will bring true purpose to your days. We push ourselves to do extra, do more, and do again. My suggestion to you is to push yourself to sink into your deeper being. Start by adding 15 minutes to your daily routine to just sit, breath, meditate, pray, and listen. Using your senses to hear, feel, smell, see, and maybe taste what is before you will ease your stress and deepen your awareness. If you are spiritual, then sit quietly and listen to the Spirit every day, and it will guide you. Awakening to your true self is a journey, but it is a journey that we need to prioritize. The destination is of no significance. Leaving go of our shallow/false self, which is our ego, will pump you to find peace and happiness. Letting go of assumptions. Letting go of taking things personally. Letting go of who the world thinks we are or should be. Spending time on finding you. Recognizing your intention of how you want to live your life will create your true purpose.

As elders, the three plagues that too often overshadow their life are loneliness, helplessness, and boredom.

The antidote to loneliness is for them to maintain a valued connection with their family and friends. Loneliness not only increases the risk of mental decline but also physical decline. Do not let them fall out of their community. Restoring companionship is about the quality of the relationships, not the quantity of people in their circle. Only sincere interest and listening to another will deepen that relationship.

The antidote to helplessness is recognizing that everyone, regardless of age or disability, has something to give to us and are also open to receiving. Once you step into your growth zone, wisdom grows. Many elders will have this wisdom that we need to recognize. Listen to them. Ask for their feedback. Ask for their help with small chores. They all can do something, even if it is only a hug and filling you with love.

The antidote to boredom is filling their weeks with unexpected and unpredictable interactions and happenings. Surprise them with small stuff. Take them on a trip to the seashore, invite friends to watch a sporting event together, or get a mani-pedi. Now look at their face. Are they smiling?

To conclude this chapter, Dr. William Thomas's story of "Caleb's Basket" resonates with all that will help fill your life. Your life needs to be filled at many different levels. When filling your basket/life with stones or the major events in your life, know that they are important, and you have worked hard to achieve them. When filling your basket/life with pebbles or your daily routines, know that while they can keep you busy, you will not allow stress to invade in. When filling your basket/life with sand or the small, unexpected pleasures, know that it is these beautiful events that inhale happiness and peace and what will create the memories and laughter in your life. When filling your basket/life with water or loving relationships, know that it is these that have truly filled you over the years. Relationships with family, friends, and the Spirit – these are what are paramount to your journey.

But all four levels of living are important. Values, gifts, passions, and purpose will help you create a life after caregiving ends. Building the courage to take the first step, based on awareness and curiosity, will be your springboard forward.

About The Author

Carmel Murphy-Kotyan has worked in the caregiving industry for over 25 years. She is a Certified Retirement Coach, certified caregiver consultant, end-of-life doula, and a certified Eden associate. She is director and owner of CMK Home Care, offering non-medical help and safety for elders in their place of residence. She is the founder of Elder Service Network, a network of service providers within the caregiving/aging industry that offers monthly educational webinars for family caregivers/partners. She is also the CEO of Hard Laughter Coaching, offering consulting services and support to family caregivers through the different stages of caregiving. She is a natural lifelong learner, a practitioner of mindfulness and of spiritual awakeness. Born and raised in Ireland, she now lives in the Boston area with her three kids and husband. For more information, feel free to contact Carmel at 781-266-8985, or visit www.cmkhomecare.net/caregiver-coaching and www.elderservicenetwork.org.

Brain Power: Keeping An Aging Brain In Shape
By Holly McFarland

Introduction

How old would you be if you didn't know how old you were? Greatest question ever! People often report feeling anywhere from five to fifteen years younger than their chronological age.

Research has shown that how people feel inside, and their expectations of their capabilities in older age, can have a greater impact on health, happiness, and even longevity than the date of their birth certificate.[1]

We all know people who have aged well – as well as those who have struggled in older age.

Do you have a role model of someone who illustrates successful aging? Maybe a parent, grandparent, relative, teacher, coach, co-worker, or a good friend who exhibits many positive aspects of aging? Someone you might hope to emulate one day? Role models help us see the kinds of lives we want to lead, as well as consider changes we might want to make. Their active lives allow us to recognize the value of keeping our brains active and engaged. They help us realize that we can become our own autobiographers – that we can step outside of who we are, look at all that is possible, and create the lives we want.

I have many role models but there are three who immediately come to mind. The first is my former husband's grandmother, Georgia, a master bridge player who also loved children and traveling. She loved traveling on cruise ships, but could only afford a couple of trips a year. So, when she was offered an opportunity to combine all these interests, she grabbed it. Yes, at the age of 80, she began her first career as a babysitter on a cruise ship! During the days she played games with the young children on board, and in the evenings enjoyed her off-time playing in bridge tournaments, all while cruising around the world.

My second role model was astronaut John Glenn, who traveled to outer space at the age of 77 for scientific research; to better understand how space travel can influence the physiological functioning of an older adult.

And my third is Ruth Ginsburg, who in her 80s was an inspiration for all women. A warrior for women's rights throughout her career, she used her intelligence and her voice to advocate for justice. Even after four bouts with cancer, she barely missed a day of work. She persisted.

All three of these individuals had a zest for living life to its fullest. They all exemplify successful aging through strong brain power: being productive, staying mentally fit, and leading a meaningful life. It is clear to me that having role models can help us strive to live successful, happy, and healthy lives as well as to find meaning and peace.

Some keys to the brain power of successful aging learned from role models include:

- **Making healthy lifestyle choices:** Diet/exercise/sleep.
- **Being open to new experiences:** Practicing curiosity.
- **Having active social lives:** Frequently meeting with friends and family and volunteering.
- **Reading:** Lifelong reading makes us sharper and more socially aware.
- **Identifying and pursuing happiness:** Finding what gives your life meaning.
- **Boosting brain power:** Keeping your mind active.

Whatever your age, now is the time to think about successful aging.

In this chapter we will look at how the brain ages and how you can reduce the negative effects of aging and keep your mind sharp. So why do some people age successfully, and others don't? Let's look at the research.

Changes In The Aging Brain

There is considerable research that debunks the myth that we will all experience failing memory in our lifetime. As a person gets older, changes do occur in all parts of the body, including the brain. According to the National Institute on Aging:

- Certain parts of the brain shrink, especially those important to learning and other complex mental activities.
- In certain brain regions, communication between neurons (nerve cells) can be reduced.
- Blood flow in the brain may also decrease

Brain scientists, however, are learning new information about the brain constantly. As we study the recent research, we are seeing a different and more uplifting picture for the human brain. That picture tells us:

- There is no such thing as "over the hill."
- While changes in the brain can affect mental function, there is growing evidence that the brain remains plastic, able to adapt to new challenges and tasks, as people age.[2]
- The brain continues to make new brain cells. This has such exciting possibilities for aging brains that brain-cell generation is now a cutting-edge area of neuroscience.

Psychologists researching the normal changes of aging have found that, although some aspects of memory and processing change as people get older, simple behavior changes can help people stay sharp for as long as possible.[3] How we live our daily lives is critical and something we can control.

Boosting Brain Power

Active aging involves more than moving your body. You also need to move your brain. "When you exercise you engage your muscles to help improve overall health," says Dr. Ipsit Vahia from Harvard-affiliated McLean Hospital. "The same concept applies to the brain. You need to exercise it with new challenges to keep it healthy."[4]

So, what can we do now to stay sharp, happy, and wise into middle and old age? There is no single secret to successful aging. Achieving the greatest outcomes, however, requires physical, mental, and social strategies and activities. Let's look at what we can do to protect our brain.

Physical Strategies: These are the lifestyle choices we make. These strategies will not only help our physical/cardio health, but they will also improve our cognitive functions like short- and long-term memory recall, problem-solving, concentration, and attention to detail.

Making healthy lifestyle choices includes:

- **Getting regular physical exercise.** This is at the top of the list because it can slow or even reverse the brain's physical decline the way it does with our muscles. Studies show that aerobic exercise is one of the most effective ways to slow the process of brain aging and may help combat changes in the brain associated with dementia. Walking has been shown to have a large and lasting effect, and there may even be a dose-response curve, such that the more you do it, the bigger the effect.[5]

- **Eating healthy foods.** A diet rich in vegetables, nuts, olive oil, berries, fish, and whole grains, also called a Mediterranean diet or Mind diet, has been shown to improve working memory and lower the risk of Alzheimer's, according to John Medina/Brain Rules for Aging Well.
- **Getting enough sleep.** Sleeping well means minimizing stress.
- **Meditating.**
- **Swimming.** A high value strategy, swimming is a physical activity with mental benefits as well. It has cardiovascular and muscle-building benefits, but also involves constant thinking and processing. This helps the life of the body and the mind.

Mental/Psychological Strategies: Mental stimulation is equally as important in boosting brainpower as we age.

Your brain has the ability to learn and grow as you age – a process called brain plasticity – but for it to do so, you must train it on a regular basis. Learning a new and demanding skill is the most scientifically proven way to reduce age-related memory decline. The brain can only create new neural pathways and connections if it is challenged to do something it doesn't already know. And so, repeating an activity or partaking in a hobby that doesn't challenge you intellectually doesn't stimulate new growth. However, when you learn, you are training your brain to think in a different way. Any activity that requires you to interact with the world and to respond to it differently each time is an activity that helps protect the brain against dementia and neural atrophy.

There are many advantages of continuing the practice of learning. Studies show that when seniors learn a new skill, such as playing an instrument, learning a new language or a new technology, it strengthens connections within the brain. The key is to plunge yourself into the deep end of learning environments every day. No exceptions. According to Dr. John Morris, director of social and health policy research at the Harvard-affiliated Institute for Aging Research, "Embracing a new activity that also forces you to think and learn and requires ongoing practice can be one of the best ways to keep the brain healthy."

Social Engagement Strategies: Humans share a fundamental need to interact with other people. According to the Global Council on Brain Health, social engagement is interacting with others, feeling connected to other people, doing purposeful activities with others, and/or maintaining meaningful social relationships.[6]

As people age, it is common that their social networks change and sometimes grow smaller. Staying socially active and maintaining your relationships are important parts of healthy aging. There is compelling evidence that social engagement has positive impacts on the brain. Older people who are more socially engaged and have larger social networks tend to have a higher level of cognitive function.

Activities To Help Keep Our Brains In Shape

What kind of activities can help us stay sharp and keep our brains in shape?

The most effective activities combine being active and having some level of stimulation; this could be walking, or some other physical exercise mixed with cognitive activities that provide some challenge to stimulate the brain. The key is trying something new that is challenging.

Let's look at some of these activities that we can do to better prepare physically, mentally, and socially for successful aging.

Physical Activities

- Walking.
- Aerobic exercise.
- Swimming.
- Meditating.
- Biking.
- Golf.
- Pickleball/tennis.
- Yoga.
- Hiking.

- Strength training.
- Dancing.

Cognitive Activities

- Learning to play a musical instrument.
- Working on brain games (puzzles and crosswords).
- Teaching something to others.
- Learning a new language or new technology.
- Writing.
- Volunteering.
- Painting.
- Starting a business.
- Going back to school.
- Reading.
- Cooking.
- Drawing.
- Painting.
- Quilting/knitting.
- Photography.
- Gardening.
- Enrolling in a course.
- Tapping into webinars and podcasts in subjects of interest.
- Learning a new skill.
- Brushing up on existing skills.

Social Activities

- Start by staying in touch with friends and family, and try to visit with them regularly, either by phone or in person.

- Make new connections by looking for new opportunities to engage with others.
- Volunteer in your community.
- Join a group focused on activities you enjoy, such as playing cards, or a book club.
- Help others, whether informally or through organizations.
- Challenge yourself by trying a new social activity you haven't tried before.
- Maintain social connections with people of different ages, including younger people.
- If already active, diversify your activities.
- Join a gym or fitness center to stay physically fit and engage with others.
- Schedule regular visits with grandkids, or volunteer at a school or children's organization.

A Plan For Keeping Your Brain In Shape

Follow these steps in putting together a plan that will help keep your brain in shape:

1. Set goals and never stop dreaming. Personal goal setting is important throughout life because it helps you find purpose and meaning.
2. Stay socially engaged with friends, family, and community groups.
3. Exercise daily, eat a nutrient-rich balanced diet, and get plenty of sleep.

4. Find a cognitive activity that you enjoy; choose something that you are passionate about and find rewarding.
5. Find an activity that is challenging. Remember, challenge creates growth. A new activity engages your brain to learn something new and create new pathways, so you are helping reduce memory decline. If you do not want to do something new, at least raise the bar for an existing activity.
6. Find an activity that is complex. A complex activity will not only spark excitement for you but will also force your brain to work on thought processes like problem-solving and creative thinking. These stimulate, challenge, and grow new neural paths.
7. Practice the activity. You have to work at improving memory since it doesn't happen automatically. Practice makes permanent. Scientists tell us that when you practice an activity, your brain's neurons are "firing" and creating new circuits, so the activity becomes habit. Neurons that "fire" together, "wire" together so the habit becomes permanent. Your activity should require some level of constant practice.
8. Strive to be positive about aging. If you feel young, your cognitive abilities improve.

By following these steps, your brain can remain plastic: ready to study, ready to explore, and ready to learn at any age.

A Meaningful Life

Memories make us who we are. It is important to understand that memory is not just for remembering. It has an important role to play in giving us meaning in our lives and is critical for our sense of who we are. Memory is powerful, for it can take us into the past, present, and future. It is through memory that we are able to look back on all that we've experienced and, at the same time, to image the future and see the person that we are yet to become. It is when we take stock of our life as a whole that we get the most meaning out of life. But we need our memory to do this.

So, now: How old would you be if you didn't know how old you were? When we use and work our brains to keep ourselves active and engaged, we can answer this question with energy and joy of living. Keeping our brains in shape and our minds sharp is as easy as following a plan with an eye toward physical, mental, and social engagement.

There is no need to fall into the "aging trap" that says our minds aren't as clear and our memories aren't as good as they were during earlier years. Leveraging our brain's plasticity, we can continue to grow and learn and live meaningful lives well into older age and look forward to that future with excitement.

About The Author

Holly McFarland is owner of HSM Consultants and a career and retirement coach with Lifelaunch Consulting. With more than 20 years of experience in career services leadership and corporate leadership development, Holly offers expertise in aligning individual, learning, and organizational objectives to achieve desired outcomes. As a retirement coach, she helps pre-retirees define and design their next chapter in life with purpose and intention. Holly received her MBA from Franklin University and holds the following coaching qualifications: certified career coach (CCI), certified retirement coach (ROC), and certified executive coach (WABC and Marshall Goldsmith Coaching). **Holly dedicates this chapter to her six grandsons, Zayden, Cam, Jack, Cooper, Maddox, and Reid, who inspire her every day to look at life the way they do – with curiosity and wonder.**

Contact her at Holly.Mcfarland5@gmail.com.

References

1. Alan Castel, *Better With Age*, New York: Oxford University, 2019.

2. "How the Aging Brain Affects Thinking," National Institute on Aging, June 20, 2020.

3. "Memory Changes in Older Adults," American Psychological Association, June 2006.

4. Daniel Levitin, *Successful Aging*, New York: Dutton, 2020.

5. "Train Your Brain," Harvard Health Publishing, March 2018.

6. "The Brain and Social Connectedness," Global Council on Brain Health, 2017.

Using Life Lessons To Create A Better Path
By John Shope

In a world starved for heroes, I consider myself a lucky man because I knew who my hero was from a very early age. It was my Dad. He was the most honest, passionate, hardworking man I have ever known, and integrity was his calling card. Throughout my life, most of the decisions I've made have been based on the basic principles my Dad always told me:

1. Do what you love.
2. Do the right thing. (You know what that is, even if you don't do it.)
3. Be accountable for your decisions and actions.

So, naturally, you'd think the reason I've spent almost 40 years in the retirement industry – and so enjoy helping people prepare and transition to their second act – is that Dad showed me the way.

But hold on – that's where the story begins.

Have I Done The Right Things?

My Dad was a success in life, love, and family, but never really found his true calling in the business world. At his funeral, the eulogist proclaimed him a "witness to his faith." His wife of 60 years, 7 children, 16 grandchildren, faith community, friends, and neighborhood surrounded him and mourned his loss.

As we launched into the sad business of decoding his will and estate, we found he had planned everything perfectly! His family would be provided for and his legacy would live on. So why am I telling this tale?

My Dad seemed to live a lot of his life in anxiety, believing he would "never have enough money," feeling he wasn't properly preparing to enable his family after he passed, and seemed to focus only on the things he hadn't done versus the things he did.

As with many of his age peers, my Dad and the men of the Greatest Generation were private people. They didn't show emotion and certainly would never ask for help, which could be construed as a sign of weakness. They were men, husbands, heads of households, leaders of their communities, and expected to be able to handle everything and anything without complaining or showing emotion. This stoic demeanor continued even with his own family. All of my siblings have been very successful in life and business due to wonderful parenting, yet we were also never allowed behind the curtain to offer praise for a job well done or advice on what could possibly be discussed or improved.

It was hard to understand. For example, after receiving my first professional job offer after college, I ran excitedly to tell my Dad and ask him what I should do. "Is this a good offer?" I asked. He gave me that same decision criteria and said, "You'll know what to do."

1. Do what you love.
2. Do the right thing. (You know what that is, even if you don't do it.)
3. Be accountable for your decisions and actions.

Wait, what?

I thought, *Is $12,750 enough to live on?* (Okay, remember this was 1982.) *Is that fair value for a college-educated young man? Should I negotiate; wait for a different offer? Why can you not discuss money with me? I need some guidance!*

Can We Talk?

I never found the answer to that question. I assume it was because he didn't want to be judged by people who didn't know his private situation, so he did not want to appear to be judging me. Or maybe he just wanted me to learn to analyze important life situations for myself and make my own decision. Either way, neither of us knew how (or were motivated) to "go to the next level" and engage in a meaningful conversation. What I needed was recognition that I was offered a job during those very depressed economic times. Maybe he could have asked me questions such as:

- What are your goals for this first job, and what do you want to accomplish?
- Will this job provide training and a good entry into the business world?

- What will you value most right now: professional training and experience or just economic benefit?
- Imagine yourself doing that job. How does it make you feel to say you represent that company? Do its values align with yours?

Why do so many of today's "experts" in their field start every interaction with a proclamation of what you should be doing according to them?

Would you like to know what my situation is? Do you know the dynamics of how I got where I am today? Are you at all interested in learning more about me before you "solve my problem"?

Parachuting in to offer guidance for a problem that you don't have any background on is certainly not the way to engage and make anyone feel comfortable opening up to you. The real lesson for me was to learn how to engage people and make them feel comfortable sharing their feelings and desires. Not in an immediate effort to try and solve, but to establish trust and open a communication line. You see, Dad had always wanted to talk and share his thoughts and experiences, but never felt comfortable doing so. Being given permission to be human allows people to share their innermost thoughts and feelings, which helps break down individual walls people encapsulate themselves in, and can be the beginning of establishing trust. Once you begin to earn someone's trust, they begin to share more freely, which allows dialogue. Once dialogue and sharing begin, you earn permission to ask more probing questions to deepen the conversation, and show the person you are interested in them and their feelings. Good and sincere questions allow people to self-examine, and become introspective:

- What motivated you to take that action?
- How did you feel when that happened?
- You seem so joyful when you are...
- When were you happiest in life?
- What makes you sad or afraid?

I learned so many life lessons from my Dad, but maybe the most important one was the one we discovered together. Once we established a different level of conversation and sharing, we learned so much more about each other in a more moving and personal context. We methodically worked through his finances and he came to realize he was actually very prepared to satisfy his commitments to care for his wife and family after his departure. To see the satisfaction in his eyes when the "math added up" was priceless for me and him, yet it was all the more sweeter due to the fact we worked though it together without judgment or anxiety. A breakthrough moment for father and son!

The Symmetry Of Life

I've tried to utilize these principles of engagement to build trust throughout my life, but nowhere are they more important than with my two wonderful daughters. My wife and I were blessed with two young women who have full appreciation for life and family. As they've grown, I've always tried to establish core beliefs and values for them to shape their lives. Of course, I always wanted to pass on the love and passion in my Dad's principles, but tried to reshape the conversation from the lessons we discovered together.

Do What You Love

People are just naturally better at doing things they enjoy. That doesn't mean you can't teach yourself to perform activities that you aren't passionate about, but when you wake up with a desire to do something, it feels good and you will make the time to do whatever it is. Yet, people don't always recognize their own strengths and passions, sometimes the entirety of life just seems to run together. Watching my daughters grow, I would always take special note of when they seemed to be fulfilled and enjoying themselves: playing an instrument, activities that required a certain physical movement, reading a book, friends who made them feel a certain way, etc.

When life decisions came calling, we'd recall those feelings of joy and try to relate them to the outcome of the impending decision. The ability to talk with them about how the effects of that decision will make them feel can help bring to life the critical factors in making the decision. No one make perfect decisions 100 percent of the time, but making a choice because you believe the outcome will be

187

fulfilling normally results in a much better outcome than making a choice because you're afraid to fail.

Do The Right Thing

There are so many ways to interpret what "the right thing" is based on your faith, community you live in, position in life, etc. I share my Dad's belief that each individual's conscience tells them what the right thing is, you know inherently the difference between right and wrong. The true test is whether you follow the path your conscience is leading you to, and that is called integrity. I believe a person's integrity is shaped by the people they are surrounded by, and becomes a result of all the experiences they've accumulated.

Talking about life's many choices with my daughters over the years (not just their own but our family's, people around us, things that happen with their friends, etc.), I would try to discuss if they felt a certain decision a person made felt to them like the right thing to do. Not in regard to the outcome, but when you look in retrospect at the alternatives that existed, did they do the right thing? Is that a decision you would have made? Why or why not? No judgment, no critique – just allowing them to express their feelings and challenge themselves and their own conscience.

Be Accountable

Many young people feel an inordinate pressure to be perfect. I certainly saw this in periods of my daughters' lives. The fear of making a bad decision can freeze them into inaction, create undo anxiety, and generally inhibit taking on new challenges for risk of failure.

When you've invested the time and energy to create trust in a relationship, and there is open dialogue about dreams and desires, I found that this third decision principle actually – though initially sounding daunting – can make the process easier. You will make many decisions in life and for so many different reasons. But if you've spent the time exploring your feelings and try to do what you love, and do the right thing, it's easy to stand up and be accountable for any decision you've made. Regardless of the outcome (and no one's perfect, remember), if you're following your heart and your conscience, be proud of your decisions and actions. The happiest and most fulfilled people I know utilize all their life learning (the good and the bad) to plot their future course and make life choices.

Retirement Transition Coaching Should Capture Peoples Spirits and Dreams

The life lessons my Dad passed to me and I have tried to implement with my daughters have simultaneously prevailed in my professional life. I've spent almost forty years in the financial retirement business trying to help people identify what their goals and dreams really are, and then to prepare financially. I view my professional retirement career as a life internship which has led me to retirement transition coaching.

Now, as a retirement transition coach, I utilize the same guiding principles to help people identify and solve not just the financial aspects of retirement, but the equally important mental, physical, and emotional well-being aspects of this most precious time of life.

Learning how to assemble a real-life action plan to provide joy and fulfillment for people transitioning into retirement has followed the same decision-making principles I've learned and used with my family:

Do What You Love

Transitioning to a new life phase like retirement is the perfect time to review your life experiences and identify what gave you excitement, happiness, and fulfillment. I like to give the clients I work with a series of exercises that ask them to recall what activities or experience made them most happy during their life. Then I ask, "What about that experience gave you the joy?" Once we pinpoint what elicited the feelings of passion, we can discover new activities to replicate that feeling.

Just like my conversations with my daughters, it always helps to have a partner or significant other work through the exercises with you. They can provide an independent view of when you seemed to "be at your best," and sometimes just help recall periods of your life. Equally, if they will be experiencing your next act with you, it is incredibly helpful to learn where your partner is going. Not every activity has to be shared together, but it will help your partnership to find some activities you can enjoy together.

Do The Right Thing

Performing life review and planning exercises in preparation for your next chapter also provides an excellent time to evaluate where you fit in your community's efforts for the greater good of mankind. When I speak of community, I mean your family, your faith, your local community, any affinity groups you belong in, and just society at large. Many of us propel through our professional working years head down and focused on our primary day-to-day functions, never really taking account of how we are affecting the world or future generations. My Dad always challenged me and all my siblings to be active contributors in the things we did. Equally, we have tried to influence our daughters to lend their voice to the causes they care about.

I urge the transitioning clients I work with that, when they have the gift of being able to take control of their time and how they will spend it during transition into retirement, they should allow themselves to consider how they may give back to society a portion of their time, treasure, and talent. It's the single best investment a person can make that will certainly pay future dividends.

Be Accountable

Holding yourself accountable is even more important in retirement transition work than ever before. When the daily routines you've applied and held to throughout your professional life suddenly disappear, your voice and conscience (and if you're lucky, that of your partner, significant other, or family) will be your north star to keep you on track. It is the sad reality of life that, as we age, many of our acquaintances begin to fade away. Throughout our daughters' younger years, there were always playgroups, school functions, and activities to constantly bring new people into our life, usually with similar interests and circumstances. Equally, in our work lives, most of us need to work with others and meet new people, which provides continual opportunities to keep a circle of friends, or at least acquaintances nearby.

When we find the freedom in retirement to control our own time and interactions, it's so important to make building our social networks and creating new interactions a priority. I grew up with a large immediate family and enough cousins and friends to make every occasion feel like a celebration. Equally, we've passed the need for community on to our daughters, encouraged them to always find their village, and be an active participant.

I encourage my retirement clients to review their social networks before transitioning in an analytical fashion. It's not a grading exercise (consider how many friends you have), rather it creates a benchmark to evaluate how you feel about your current circumstance. If you feel good about your network, then what can we do to ensure it stays intact. If you'd like to expand your current network, we can brainstorm new ways to expand your social circle by finding activities and causes you care about, which is the easiest way to find people of like mind to add to your network.

Retirement Transition Coaching – Why We Do This

Helping individuals preparing for the most significant transition in their life is a privilege, something not to be taken lightly. Working through a process of helping people identify lifelong passions, dreams, and goals is a gift to both them and you.

About The Author

John Shope began his mission to help people transition into a satisfying retirement while working as a successful sales and marketing leader in the corporate retirement industry with some of the largest financial services firms in the United States for over 35 years. His lifelong passion for coaching and mentoring individuals, in addition to his advanced degree, professional certifications, and retirement planning experience, naturally led him to the retirement transition coaching industry. John believes that previewing your retirement life while still in your working years allows you to clarify your life goals and desired purpose while forming the habits to keep your mind and body active, and creating strategies to solidify your personal network. He says that in retirement, the best thoughts start with," I am glad I did" and not "I wish I had." He believes that working with a professional retirement transition coach for your "retirement test drive" can spur you into action now, so that you're prepared for life's most wonderful ride – your retirement! John can be reached at jfshope1@gmail.com.

The Three Most Important Things
To Know Before You Go
By Judi Snyder

And the survey says, "I want to know my loved ones will be taken care of." What was the survey? The survey asked one simple question – "What gives you peace of mind?" – and that was the number one answer. I was shocked it wasn't about money. Being in financial services, I am constantly hearing my clients express fear about running out of money in retirement. And while that is certainly a major concern, it takes a back seat to "knowing their loved ones will be fine." My challenge was to figure out exactly what "taken care of" meant. With such an ambiguous statement, it could mean a whole host of things from leaving your loved ones a legacy of money, vacation homes, or family heirlooms.

The truth is no one wants their loved ones to suffer and they know that upon their departure from this world there will be grief. Most people want to minimize that grief as much as possible. The best way to do that is to make decisions that may be difficult for those you love, ahead of time, so your loved ones do not have to make them in times of intense crisis and mourning. According to Dr. Janel Phillips, PhD, of The Henry Ford Health System, most people will experience "grief brain" during and after the loss of a loved one. Grief brain can impact all our emotional and mental functions, including areas within the limbic system and pre-frontal cortex. These involve emotional regulation, memory, multi-tasking, organization, and learning. When these circumstances converge, your brain function takes a hit. Phillips goes on to say that if you're overwhelmed with grief, it stands to reason that you won't absorb your environment the same way you would when you're content. By making important decisions before you depart to the heavens, you are giving the greatest parting gift to your loved ones: the gift of not making emotional and potentially permanent and regretful decisions while in a state of a temporary cognitive impairment.

After working with hundreds of clients, three key areas became apparent – one of which may surprise you!

- Forgiveness and Spiritual Discussion
- Money Matters
- Important Documents

Forgiveness

Much to my surprise, this was the most prevalent and emotional area by far. How did I arrive at this epiphany? Having remembered a quote I heard – "I wish life had a rewind button" – I asked another simple question: "What is your number one rewind moment"? Most all the answers I received were about forgiveness and conversations that never happened. Sometimes the forgiveness was not forgiving another person, rather forgiving ourselves for mistakes in the past.

Forgiving ourselves is *the* most difficult of all. If you are unable to forgive yourself, you will not be able to fully forgive others. Forgiveness is a choice. Forgiveness requires empathy, compassion, kindness, and understanding.

The best way to forgive yourself for anything is to reframe the "mistake." I recommend 3 steps, the triple A's, to reframing mistakes:

Adopt the philosophy that "things happen for me, not to me. Mistakes are about detours. You wouldn't hold a grudge the rest of your life for making a wrong turn on a road trip, so why are you doing this with your life's decisions? Sometimes these detours help you discover the unknown beauty you would have otherwise missed with monocular vision. Looking for the gold in any mistake is paramount to moving through the process of forgiving. Rarely do we get anything right the first time. Innovation and invention are born out of mistakes. America was discovered by a ship being only degrees off course! Embrace the detours with curiosity and as a nudge to change course and look for the gold.

Advise within your self-talk as though you are teaching a small child. I'm willing to bet you wouldn't speak to a child the way you speak to yourself. A great way of practicing positive inner-speak is by taking a picture of your 5-year-old self and having an out-loud conversation about the "mistake" and how or what might have been learned from that mistake. Most everyone is compassionate to children; we are harshest to our ourselves. This exercise helps tame our inner critic and gives us the space and permission to reframe the experience.

Acknowledge the gold that was born from the "mistake." Look back and review what you may have missed had you not made the mistake? Many people can look back at a bad marriage mistake and acknowledge the blessing of their children that would not have come had they married someone else. Some mistakes aren't so obvious, but there is always gold in every mishap.

Forgiving others is not easy by any means, but we are able to forgive others more easily than ourselves. To forgive those who hurt you can significantly improve both psychological well-being and physical health. Forgiveness is not about letting go and moving on from harm done to you from someone. It is not about forgiving the "act" against us or excusing the person that committed the act. Forgiveness is about acknowledging that person as a fallible human being who made a mistake because something inside of them was wounded. It is not about you. Let me repeat, *it is not about you!* Hurt people hurt. By forgiving others you break the cycle.

Anger causes stress and prolonged stress can lead to heart disease among other health ailments. In a study about forgiveness and stress, Loren L. Toussaint found that when forgiveness rose, levels of stress went down. Reduced stress, in turn, led to a decrease in mental health and physical symptoms.

If you are old enough to read this book, then chances are you've harbored a grudge or two in your life. I know I have. Here is the good news for grudge holders, we can learn to forgive. That's right, forgiveness is a learned behavior.

The first step toward forgiveness is to have empathy for the person you want to forgive. We can use the Triple A approach with others just as we used for our self. We can adopt the philosophy that if this person is doing something to us then there is something for us to learn from this event. We can look at that person with compassion and recognize that their inner child has been wounded and we can usually, in hindsight, see some gift that arose from being hurt by that person. If we practice with strangers, we can get better when we want to forgive those closest to us. We've all had experiences with customer service people who seem more like the "sales prevention" department, then customer service or the server at a restaurant that is curt. Their attitude toward us rarely has anything to do with us personally. They may be having a bad day, or they just may be an unhappy person, but it is not about us. If we practice with the small situations, then the bigger situations become easier. Forgiveness is a muscle that needs to be exercised. Just like working out any other muscle, you can't expect to be buff overnight. Forgive the small things before the ginormous things. Be patient and compassionate with yourself in this process. If forgiveness was easy, there would be no war. It is not easy, but it is necessary for happiness and well-being.

Spiritual Discussion

"Things left unsaid and the courage to express my feelings" is one of the top five regrets dying people lament. Difficult conversations are, well, difficult. It is difficult to have a conversation about dying with a person battling cancer or a parent in their eighties. It is difficult to speak of death when someone is fighting for their life. It is the unknown which make us uncomfortable to approach the subject since we have no experience to speak of. We like to stick to what we "think" we know. Difficult conversations about the spiritual hereafter are riddled with unknowns, so we tell ourselves "we'll get around to having that death conversation," but that time never comes. There is a plethora of research proving that people would rather stay in horrific and abusive situations because it is "familiar" rather than the unknown. If you knew with certainty that having those difficult "unknown" conversations would bring you and those you love peace of mind, would you consider the discussion?

In the *Journal of American College of Surgeons*, Dr. Christina Puchalski has developed a tool for spiritual discussion to better identify the spiritual needs of patients, and I recommend we use the same tool for our discussion with loved ones.

By having spiritual discussion, you gift your loved ones with the permission to discuss issues of importance to them without judgment. Puchalski uses an acronym, FICA (Faith, Importance, Community, Address). I've added to her model and summarized in the following:

F represents *faith*—Do you consider yourself religious or spiritual? Do you have a faith? What gives meaning to your life? Do you believe in life after death, reincarnation, resurrection, etc.

I represents *importance*—Is your spiritual belief important in your life? How do you want to integrate your belief in the memory of your loved ones?

C represents *community*—Are you part of a spiritual or faith community? How do you want to be remembered by that community and who do you want to participate in memorial services? Do you want burial or cremation?

A represents *address*–How can your loved ones and healthcare providers address and respect your wishes in the care and handling of your affairs before and after you pass?

Spirituality is an important, if not essential, component of each person's overall well-being. Spirituality is a dynamic and ongoing issue; readdress it over time. Keep in mind this is about your loved one, and be cautious not impose your beliefs onto others. One of the most difficult conversations to have with your loved ones is about death, but I promise you, it will prove to be one of the most comforting and healing when you or your loved one passes. I experienced this opportunity, or what I consider to be a blessing, when my beloved mother was dying of brain cancer. We would talk for hours about life after death. We even joked at times about what her "sign" would be; a sign that would allow me to know unequivocally she was with me in spirit. She passed in 1992 at the too-young age of 53, and those conversations have healed me immensely, beyond expectation over these years. I have peace of mind knowing there was nothing left unsaid, her wishes were carried out and I continue to appreciate our predetermined "signs" that pop up on a regular basis to remind me she is with me, guides me, and lives on in my heart.

You don't want to have your loved ones ruminating on the mind-numbing *what-ifs* and *maybes*. Having these difficult conversations will allow you to relish in the delight of your happy memories and heal. You may even consider making video's and writing a book so your "soul legacy" can be passed on for generations.

Money Matters

Have a plan to replace your income for your partner or spouse. If you are married or have a partner and your lifestyle is dependent on two incomes, the loss of one of those incomes can be catastrophic. You don't want your loved one having to deal with "survival" during their time of grief.

Have a plan for long-term care because no plan is still a plan. You don't want to rely on family, friends, or the government. The number one reason most people don't buy traditional long-term care insurance is they don't want to pay a premium for something they may not use. However, there is a higher probability and higher risk financially and emotionally that you'll need long term care rather than other risks you are already insuring for, like homeowners and auto insurance.

Another reason retirees don't pursue a long-term care plan is they believe they can't qualify medically, or the price will be astronomical! While that may have been true in the past, there are now new products that address these challenges.

Important Documents

As a retirement and transition consultant, I am often called when someone passes on to assist in end-of-life matters. Whether a person passes from an anticipated illness or unexpectedly, the shock is just as earth shattering. Regardless of the reason of the passing of a loved one, anticipated illness, suicide or sudden illness, or accident, there is a gamut of emotions that take over the ability to focus and rationally deal with the burial and closing of the estate. The emotions range from guilt from the relief that your loved one isn't suffering, to anger to shock, and many times a combination of all. Having a "brain trust" or financial team, and your personal papers and documents organized, is one of the best gifts you can give your loved ones at a time when they are least able to make solid decisions.

Remember the "grief brain" earlier, that kicks in fast and furiously.

Develop a list of your "brain trust" team with contact info such as best phone numbers, addresses, and emails. The team may include estate planning attorneys, insurance agents, financial advisors, CPAs/accounting professionals, bankers, and other financial institutions. Be sure and have this list at the top of the file. Designate a known location such as a file cabinet, safe, or safe deposit box, and discuss this file with several people you trust.

Next, you will want to organize your important documents, so they are easily accessed by your loved ones to discuss with your brain trust team. I recommend organizing these documents in the following four categories:

1. Estate Planning
2. Insurance
3. Investments
4. Personal

If you have not done estate planning, please consider making this a priority. Many people have the misconception that if they don't have a lot of money, they do not need an estate plan. Having a plan protects you from others or the "state" making decisions you don't agree with regarding your end-of-life wishes, or the estate you worked hard to build during your life. I cannot stress enough how difficult it becomes for your loved ones to make tough unanimous decisions about your end-of-life wishes.

Many times, families are torn apart by the difference in interpretation of your wishes. Make your desires clear and have the discussion with everyone's attendance. Your estate planning file may include documents such as:

a. Advance Directive
b. Living Will
c. Durable and Financial Power of Attorney
d. Healthcare Proxy
e. Pre-Paid Burial
f. Information for Obituary

Unlike previous generations, insurance can have a multitude of uses. It was once assumed that you bought life insurance to protect your non-earning or low-earning spouse from the loss of income upon an early unanticipated death. Transferring the risk to an insurance company can help "insure your retirement paycheck." Be sure your beneficiaries are up to date on all your insurance products! Your insurance file may include documents such as:

a. Life Insurance Policies
b. Long-Term Care Policies
c. Annuities
d. Home and Vehicle Insurance

Investments can be confusing on a good day, let alone when you are in the throes of grief. There are endless ways to invest your money and endless professionals that offer investments. You may have more than one investment advisor on your team. You will want to label each investment with the advisor contact information specific to that investment so your loved ones are not contacting the incorrect custodian, which can result in letting fees accrue or lapse, or proceed checks mailed to incorrect addresses. Again, just as with insurance, be sure your beneficiaries are up to date on all your investment products! Your investments file may include documents such as:

a. Brokerage Accounts
b. Self-Directed Investment Accounts
c. Online Security Accounts
d. Investment Clubs
e. Stock Certificates
f. Bonds
g. Alternative Investments (Oil and Gas, Real Estate, Precious Metals)
h. Pension Plan
i. Profit Sharing and Purchase Plan Documents
j. Retirement Plans like 401k, 403b, 457, IRA, SEP IRA, and Roth IRA
k. Bank Records, Safe Deposit Information and Keys, and CDs (Certificates of Deposit)

Personal is likely where everything else will be filed. Your personal file should be updated on a regular basis and should act as your "working" file that is utilized daily. Your personal file may include information such as:

a. Social Security Information
b. Home Property and Vehicle Deeds

c. Tax Records
d. Military Records
e. Passwords to online accounts including social media
f. Safe Combination and Keys
g. Passports and a copy of your Driver's License
h. Credit Card Information
i. Jewelry, Collectibles and other Valuables Receipts and Records
j. Anything else you deem important!

Dealing with Debt

Debt is hard to deal with when you are alive and can be even more overwhelming for your loved ones when you are gone. There are a couple of areas I want to highlight regarding the closing of an estate. I see 90 percent of confusion arising from these two areas. The closing of credit cards and debt repayment from the deceased.

Closing Credit Cards

Most people frantically close out their loved one's credit cards without the knowledge that only the person whose social security number was used to obtain the credit is responsible for any balance owed on that credit card. Even if you are an "authorized" user of the credit card, but your credit was not used to obtain the credit line, you are not required to pay the balance. I've seen far too many newly widowed clients put themselves in debt by paying on a credit card they are not responsible for at a time when half or sometimes three quarters of their income has ended. I recommend reviewing each credit card you own in which you have a designated authorized user. Determine whose credit was used to obtain that credit card and notate that on the file folder where you file your statements. This will make the process of closing them out go smoothly for your loved ones and it can make all the difference in the world to their financial situation.

Closing Of An Estate

The closing of an estate can be daunting for your loved ones. A conversation about your debt prior to your passing can help mitigate or eliminate estate debt in advance. Depending on the amount of debt, you may strongly consider seeking legal help to resolve an insolvent estate, since there are several legal statutes governing who should be paid and how much. According to www.debt.org details vary by state, but in general only after arranging to resolve all debts, can you distribute assets to heirs. An estate must pay debts in the following order of priority:

1. Funeral expenses
2. Estate administration costs
3. Taxes
4. Other general debts which can be vague and may need legal expertise

If the estate owes more than it is worth, it is considered "insolvent." When an estate is insolvent (or near-insolvent), negotiation for debt forgiveness is very common, since the debtholders may end up with nothing if they don't agree to a lesser amount.

Debt Forgiveness

Debt forgiveness is common for some debts to be completely or partially forgiven after death, especially if the creditor believes that the estate may not have enough money to pay all debts, and that if the creditor doesn't agree to forgive some of the debt, the other creditors will be paid first and there may not be enough money left at the end to pay to anything to the creditor at all.

When some or all a debt is "forgiven," that means that the person to whom the money was owed has agreed to reduce the size of the debt. You should get any such agreements in writing. You should also be aware that the amount forgiven is considered taxable income to the estate, and that big corporations such credit card companies will almost certainly report these amounts to the IRS.

Of course, few creditors are going to volunteer to forgive their amounts; you will need to negotiate with them if you wish to get anything reduced. If you have hired a probate attorney, this may be something you delegate to them, since they're used to it.

According to www.estateexec.com, the list of exempt assets varies by state, but two major assets are exempt everywhere: retirement savings and life insurance policies. Those two assets can be distributed to beneficiaries without regard to debts owed by the deceased.

Some states designate other entities as exempt so it's wise to check the laws where you live. Florida, for example, says the surviving spouse or children has the right to exempt household furniture and appliances up to a value of $10,000 as well as two automobiles.

Assets that are non-exempt, meaning available to be liquidated and used to pay off debts, would include a house, car, boat, bank account, artwork, stamp or coin collection, or anything that has enough value to be sold.

We can all agree that no one escapes this world alive. And when the inevitable arrives, who is best positioned to make those final decisions concerning your legacy? You! By addressing these three most important areas you will be giving your loved ones (and you) the ultimate parting gift – peace of mind!

About The Author

Twenty-seven years as a medical sales executive led Judi to realize that corporate life was unfulfilling! In 2004, she transitioned from employee to entrepreneur into financial services. Because of her own transition, Judi understands the unique challenges that come along with creating a new identity and purpose. She became a CeFT® (Certified Financial Transitionist®) to further expand her solutions for those going through financial transition and address the financial aspects of transition. She helps clients navigate through the nonfinancial aspects of retirement, such as finding purpose, exploring spirituality, and health and wellness, which are as important as the financial planning yet rarely addressed. Becoming a CPRC (Certified Professional Retirement Coach) expanded her tool chest to holistically guide those in or approaching retirement. Happiness and fulfillment are about more than the money. She can be reached at Judi@HomeStretchFinancial.com or HomeStretchFinancial.com

Random Acts Of Kindness
By Michele Fantt Harris

All across the world — in the midst of uncertain and challenging times — there is reassuring and inspiring evidence that kindness can and will always prevail. I am writing this during the summer of 2020, at the height of the coronavirus pandemic, and I am uplifted daily by the ways in which people are helping each other cope — how they are offering random acts of kindness to their neighbors and their communities. Through these acts of kindness, many retirees, in particular, have gained an increased self-awareness of what "purpose and fulfillment" means to them.

Doing Good Is Good For Your Health

Performing a random act of kindness is as good for you as it is for the recipient. "Doing good," as the saying goes, helps you stay engaged and inspired during your retirement. Have you ever noticed that when you do something nice for someone, you feel better too? I know that I do. I volunteer several times a year at Keswick Nursing Home in Baltimore, where I conduct the worship service. Although I always receive accolades from the residents (and I truly do this work for them and not for myself), I inevitably leave the facility more inspired and energized then when I came.

Why does doing something nice (i.e., being altruistic) feel so good? Well, it's partially biological. Doing nice things for others boosts the body's levels of serotonin, the neurotransmitter responsible for feelings of satisfaction and well-being. Like exercise, altruism releases endorphins, a phenomenon known as a "helper's high."(1) This elated state generates feelings of satisfaction and gratitude. And it drives us to want to be kind, generous or altruistic again.

The health benefits of kindness go far beyond a "feel good" sensation. Doing good for others actually changes the body in positive, long-term ways. **Kindness eases anxiety**. A study on happiness from the University of British Columbia showed that social anxiety is associated with low positive affect (PA). Positive affect refers to an individual's experience of positive moods, such as joy, interest, and alertness. The researchers found that participants who engaged in kind acts displayed significant increases in PA.(2)

Kindness is also good for your heart. Kindness releases the hormone oxytocin (sometimes referred to as the "cuddle hormone"), which expands the blood vessels in your heart and lowers your blood pressure. Kindness strengthens your heart physically and emotionally.

Kindness — which has a multitude of benefits for doer and recipient alike — can help you live longer. Being kind reduces stress in your life. Doing good leads to your personal happiness and will motivate you to do good again. I happen to believe that performing regular "random acts of kindness" may be the secret formula to a healthy, happy retirement!

Starting Your Acts Of Kindness

You might be thinking, "I need to get started," or "I need to do more." The best way to get started with a deliberate practice of "acts of kindness" is to begin with something you love to do: a passion, a hobby, or an interest. What do you enjoy doing? What things do you do well?

Do you enjoy cooking or baking? Prepare a meal for someone who is confined. Prepare a lunch or feast for hospital workers. Bring treats to your local fire station. Bake cookies or cupcakes for your mail carrier. Prepare snacks or treats for children and working parents in your neighborhood who might not often have extra time to bake or cook — or who don't have your unique talent for lemon bars or baked macaroni and cheese.

If you love creating surprises and supporting local businesses, why not combine the two interests? Treat your family and friends to an impromptu dinner delivery from their favorite restaurant! In some states, you're even able to get cocktails delivered with the food. This kind of "dinner surprise" allows you to do a good deed by supporting a local restaurant and giving your family and friends a welcomed break from cooking. This kind of surprise can be particularly appreciated by busy friends who are full-time caretakers for their children, spouses, or parents.

Do you like to talk and communicate with others? Do you miss the social chit chat that you used to enjoy at work? Reach out to a friend, family member or neighbor who is experiencing loneliness or isolation. Call a church member who is listed on the church's sick and shut-in list. Call a friend who you haven't spoken to for a long time. Reach out to your children or other family members and tell them how much you love and appreciate them. Tell a recent high school or college graduate that you're proud of their accomplishments and encourage them as they begin the next chapter of their life.

The pandemic taught me something that we can all use forever as part of our "random acts of kindness" practice — sharing low-cost experiences like seeing a movie together can be truly meaningful for all. On weekends during the summer, my husband and I join our young neighbors and their children to watch movies on an outdoor screen. Each family brings their own snacks and later we discuss the movie. The ages in our "neighborhood movie date night" range from 4 to 70, but we all enjoy the time to gather and watch the movie. We started this tradition as a "socially distanced" way to enjoy some activity during the 2020 pandemic, but intend to keep up the tradition long into the future. How can you go to the movies with someone soon? Whether you physically attend a movie together or whether you simply call someone you know and watch a movie or a favorite television show together — with the phone line between you open so you can talk and laugh — these simple, low-cost shared experiences can bring us a lot of joy.

Perhaps you're not a great talker, so delivering kindness via phone calls or face-to-face visits feels taxing to you. That's okay! Send a text or a card to someone who needs a random act of kindness. Send a motivational or heartfelt text to a friend who is lonely. Text someone a joke or a funny picture to cheer them up. Make a card out of construction paper, add pictures to it and write an inspirational message before sending the card to someone who lives alone or in a nursing home.

Do you love to read? Next time you read an interesting article in the newspaper or magazine, don't just set it down and forget about it. Clip it out and send it to a friend. And when you finish reading a good book, don't just put it on a shelf. Send the book to a friend who isn't able to get out, or donate the book to your local library or neighborhood association — so that others may enjoy a good read. (You can even write a little note inside the book to tell its next reader that you hope they enjoy the book as much as you did.) Sharing what we're reading can bring people who are far away back together in spirit. If you have a childhood friend who lives far away but might feel nostalgic about what's happening where you live, send your old chum an article of interest from your town's local newspapers. Make sure your article is inspirational and uplifting. Don't just send them the obituaries of other old friends!

If you love reading and you love making other people delighted, consider building a "little free library" in your front yard or the lobby of your condo or apartment building, if allowed. Put books in it for your neighbors to borrow, and invite them to donate their books. Learn how to build and install one, and how to get started at LittleFreeLibrary.org. Another great way to bring learning and leisure to others is to organize a donation drive for coloring books and toys for a daycare center or hospital pediatric ward.

Are you an animal lover? Help at a veterinarian's office, or assist a disabled neighbor or friend by walking their dog. Could you make someone's life easier by giving their dog a bath, brushing it, or driving it to its next vet appointment? You could even start a dog walking business for those neighbors who are working during the day. You and the dogs will both appreciate the exercise! Also, consider volunteering at your local animal shelter, where you can bring toys, donate old blankets, sheets, and towels, or go play with and comfort the animals.

If you really love animals and the outdoors and live in a rural area, volunteer at a local farm or ranch. Take care of the horses and other animals by feeding them and cleaning their enclosures and equipment. Plant and pick vegetables and fruit. Buy the farm-grown fruits and vegetables and donate the food to a family in need or to your local homeless shelter or food bank.

Even More Ways To Deliver Random Acts Of Kindness

Don't forget about our uniformed service men and women who are serving and protecting our country. Write letters or send inspirational messages and care packages to soldiers, sailors, airmen, marines, or coastguardsmen at home and abroad.

Although we live in a land of plenty, there are many who are less fortunate. Take time to help those who are in a homeless shelter. Cook a meal and serve it to the residents. Not a cook? Have pizzas or a prepared meal delivered to the shelter. Spend the day talking to those experiencing homelessness or cleaning the shelter facility to make it more comfortable. Give money or a free meal to the men, women, and children you see on the streets. Sign up for a weekly shift at your local soup kitchen. Donate your old eyeglasses to charity. Donate your slightly used clothes, shoes, and furniture to your local homeless or domestic violence shelter. Knit or crochet the shelter residents a homemade blanket or scarf. Volunteer by teaching classes about anything you have expertise in, which might be helpful – like how to interview for a job or how to remain positive when times are difficult.

Are you a nature lover who enjoys being outdoors? Buy flowers to hand out to strangers or send to a nursing home or a hospital. Plant a tree or donate a tree planting at a neighboring park or school. Water a neighbor's grass and flowers. Rake the leaves or mow the lawn for those who are elderly or disabled.

Feed the birds in the park. Live in a cold climate? Scrape the ice off a neighbor's windshield or shovel the snow from their driveway. Donate and encourage your friends to sponsor you as you walk or run in a charity 5k race.

Enjoy volunteering at your local school or public library? Offer to read to a classroom during story time or volunteer to help a student learn to read. Tutor a struggling student. Offer to do chores for a teacher who doesn't have a teaching assistant. Create a new bulletin board for a classroom. Raise money for a school project or buy an item on a teacher's classroom wish list. At your local library, volunteer at story time and invite other retired friends to be readers as well. Always donate your used books and CDs — especially to libraries in underserved neighborhoods.

Play a musical instrument or have a dramatic flair? Perform a concert at a retirement home. Attend a dance recital or sporting event of a friend's child or grandchild. Teach others how to play a musical instrument. Organize a community choir or start a local theater troupe and perform for churches and local community groups. Many years ago, I organized a church theater group, the Union Players, which helped raise needed funds and is still active today with members whose ages range from 25 to 80!

Don't just help the people you know – give of your time and resources to strangers. Talk to a stranger at a party who looks like they don't know anyone.

Put coins in an expired parking meter and save a stranger a parking ticket! Pay for a stranger's meal at a restaurant. Write a thank you note to your mail carrier. Take time to write a letter of commendation for a salesperson who was particularly helpful to you. Share your coupons with others in the store. Take time to assist visitors who look lost in your city or town. Help an elderly or disabled person carry groceries to their car. Pay for someone's bus, cab or rideshare (e.g., Uber). Volunteer at your local English as a Second Language (ESL) class or a local GED (high school equivalency degree) program.

Have a special talent or area of expertise? Lend your services on a pro bono basis. Are you an attorney? Most state and local bar associations sponsor pro bono legal programs for persons in the community seeking legal assistance. If you are a marketing and communications guru, offer a few hours of complimentary consultation to a new start-up business or nonprofit association. Grassroots organizations are always seeking assistance with graphic design, copy writing, marketing strategy, digital communication, media relations and other forms of communication. Skilled with computers or other electronic communication? Your expertise is needed in businesses as well as in the homes of families with children and the elderly. Donate your unused electronic devices and teach others how to use the technology.

Nearly 50 years ago, The O'Jays sang the song "For the Love of Money" (with the memorable chorus *"money, money, money, money, money!"*). The song — and the idea of money as a gift — remains popular today. Give someone a gift card that you don't intend to use. Buy toys and clothes throughout the year and donate them to an orphanage. Pay for someone's dry cleaning. Pay for an elderly or disabled person's house cleaning. Pay the highway toll for the car behind you. Donate to a friend's favorite charity in their name. Give money to your alma mater. Start a scholarship at your local college or university in honor or memory of a loved one or friend. Donate money to the "underdog" candidate in the local or state election. Give money to a faith-based organization, even one that's not your own. Pay for several children in an underserved community to attend a concert or play, or pay the registration for them to attend summer camp.

Apply Kindness To Yourself Too

In all your efforts to deliver kindness to the world around you, don't forget to give yourself a little kindness too. Treat yourself to a manicure, pedicure, or spa treatment. Take time to do an activity that you love – like reading a long book or painting, or completing crafts or carpentry projects. Being kind to yourself will give you more energy and love to give to others!

About the Author

Michele Fantt Harris is EVP, HR, for the National Cooperative Bank in Arlington, VA. Michele is a Certified Retirement Coach and a Certified Career Management Coach through The Academies, Inc. She received her BA from the University of Maryland Baltimore County, an MAS from Johns Hopkins University, and a JD from the University of Baltimore. A certified HR expert, Michele teaches at Prince George's Community College and Catholic University, and serves on the Board of Regents at the Leadership Center for Excellence. This is Michele's 7th anthology contribution; her latest book, *Imagination@Work*, was released in 2019. Contact Michele at Michele.Harris19@gmail.com.

References

1. Mirele Mann, "7 Scientific Facts About the Benefit of Doing Good," Goodnet, January 26, 2017, https://www.goodnet.org/articles7-scientific-facts-about-benefit-doing-good#

2. Maile Proctor, "6 Science-Backed Ways Being Kind is Good for Your Health," September 9, 2019, https://www.quietrev.com/6-science-backed-ways-being-kind-si-giid-fir-your-health/

Don't Retire Retirement, Modernize It
By Robert Laura

Call me old fashioned, but I don't feel this deep-rooted need or a strong conviction in my core to get rid of the word retirement. I realize I am in the minority of people who think this way because almost every time I start a retirement conversation, presentation, or workshop, people are quick to chime in and tell me how the current definition doesn't even come close to fitting into what it means to people today.

Now, don't get me wrong. I fully support a new era and approach to life after work. One where a more modern set of guidelines, norms, thoughts, and feelings re-define it, especially when compared to 20 or 30 years ago. However, I think a metamorphosis is already underway and the concept of retirement is already taking on a new meaning, similar to how other popular words and phrases have changed over time.

For example, when you were growing up, did certain words and phrases mean something different when compared to today? When I was younger, and someone mentioned:

- A cloud, it was about the weather, outdoor conditions, or laying on the grass and finding fun shapes in the sky. Not the invisible place where your online data, software, or apps are stored and accessed.

223

- Something viral was a form of illness and may even be considered contagious. Now, it's the art of becoming very popular by circulating media quickly from person to person on the internet.
- Unplugging was to eliminate the flow of electricity to a television, lamp, or other appliance. Today, it means avoiding the use of any digital or electronic devices for a period of time.
- A friend was someone you were close to, saw on a regular basis, and did things together with. Currently, it's pretty much a broad range of contacts that you have varying degrees of relationships with on a social-networking website.
- Taking a "swipe" at someone was to direct criticism towards someone or something. Now, it's when you slide your fingers across a screen or pay with a credit card.
- A text was a physical book or other form of literature that you read or studied. Today, it's the primary way that people communicate with others, so they don't have to talk to them.
- A tweet was a chirping sound that came from a bird. Currently, it's a short message about what someone is doing or thinking.

This is just a small list of general word and concept changes that have taken place in the last couple of decades, and I'm sure you could come up with a few of your own. The point I am trying to make is that we don't have to eliminate the word, we just have to enhance or expand it, to more closely fit how people think, feel, and act once they reach it.

Along those lines, I also don't think it's necessary to create a crafty play of the term to symbolize that change is underway. Like many of you, I've heard everything from rewirement, arrivement, rehirement, second act, third act, encore life, and the list goes on. While I don't think these terms independently fit the new-age definition of retirement either, collectively they are an important part of redefining the term because it helps broaden the number of factors that can, and need to be included in the new definition.

As many of you know, the current, stated definition of "retirement" or "retire" means to withdraw or to cease working. So, the idea that people can rewire to focus on something else or get hired for a different career helps carve out new aspects of life in retirement.

Furthermore, I think we need to look at the history of the term to provide some additional perspective. In the early 20th century, the concept was created to get people out of the workplace. Aging workers were slowing down assembly lines, taking extra sick and leave time, and getting hurt on the job, so organizations needed a way to get them out and move younger people in.

This shouldn't be a big surprise as during those times people had been working physically demanding jobs since they were 10-12 years old, sometimes for 50-60 hours a week, and as many as 26 days a month. I don't know about you, but I get tired just thinking about this type of lifestyle. But here's the thing, the term began to change in the 1940s and '50s during what I would consider the gold watch era.

A popular tradition initiated first by the Pepsi Company in the 1940's under the guise that "you gave us your time, now we are giving you ours," this approach put a positive spin on retirement. It helped make it a cherished, time-honored tradition, symbolic of the hard work and dedication individuals made to their company after 30 or 40 years of work.

In addition to changes like these, society has made some great strides in other retirement areas. For example, employers have eliminated mandatory retirement ages, introduced phased retirement, and recognize that aging workers are an asset.

These factors are what made retirement a highly respected and celebrated phase of life to reach, and a major reason why people still consider retirement one of their biggest goals. This is a point we can't ignore. People of all ages still dream and plan on reaching a point in their life where they don't have to go to a 9-5 job. In other words, people still want to retire.

In fact, as many of you know there is a big F.I.R.E movement. That stands for Financial Independence, Retire Early. The interesting thing about the movement is that it's not about stopping work forever, but rather, taking control of your financial life and having options as to how, when, and where you want to have an impact on others (or work). So, if we just up and eliminate it, it would change one of the most important things that people are working toward.

At the heart of the matter is that as more and more Boomers reach retirement and leave the workplace, they only have a financial plan to fall back on. They aren't prepared to replace their work identity, fill their time, stay relevant and connected, as well as mentally and physically active. They just assume all of that will fall into place, but it doesn't.

Furthermore, as this group and future generations are reaching traditional retirement ages and asset levels that would allow them to retire, they are realizing their gas tank is still plenty full. They're not coasting into work on fumes like previous generations, and true to their form and efforts in the 1960s and '70s, Boomers want to make an impact!

All told, the this is one reason why I think we can continue to adjust the meaning of retirement by making it plural and adding an "s" to it. Right away, this plural version of retirement solves a number of issues.

First, it makes the decision to retire from something much easier. Right now, the decision to retire is one of the most stressful things people put themselves through. They rack their brains, run all the numbers, and waste a lot of time and energy trying to prepare for everything that might come up. They worry if they will have enough money, what they will do with their time, how they will make an impact, how they will spend all day with their spouse, and so on.

By acknowledging the idea that each of us may have multiple retirements during our lifetime, the burden is removed from making this huge, one-time, make or break decision. This new mindset says, "What's next?" instead of "I am no longer a productive part of society." It fosters positive thinking and gives Boomers permission to be proactive as they transition from one role or situation into the next.

Think about that new definition: A proactive transition from one role or situation into the next.

It doesn't hold anyone back or label them as old or done. Instead, it empowers people to look and think ahead.

This is timely because some Boomers are being pushed into retirement earlier than anticipated. They are three or five years away from their expected retirement date and are suddenly laid off, downsized, or their company closes. And because of their proximity to traditional retirement age, along with outdated beliefs about retirement, they struggle with what to do. Should they officially retire or keeping plugging along?

While there are no easy answers to a retirement decision, this new line of thinking will cause people facing this situation as well as others to change the way people talk about retirement. Instead of asking someone, "Are you retired?" we will be asking, "Is this your first, second, or third retirement?"

This is important because right now, many people think it's a good thing to fail at retirement because it indicates that they are still relevant and needed in the work world. Well, the new approach to retirement allows us to remove the idea of associating failure with someone who still wants to have an impact or spend time doing things that are important to them – at any age.

At the core of my message is the reality that retirement doesn't eliminate work, it simply re-orients it. Instead of going to the office or doing certain tasks, new retirees still need to work on themselves, their health, relationships, identity, purpose and more, all of which is already happening. Nobody who has worked with me in developing a retirement plan for at least the last 20 years has come into my office and said their goal was to sit around and do nothing for the next 30 years.

There is no doubt that retirement can mean different things to different people, and is already starting too. So, let's not find another way to divide this country, and instead continue to alter the definition of retirement so that like words other words and phrases that have changed over time, we can

229

deliver a new and fresh perspective to future generations when they are ready to move on from their primary careers.

Therefore, the word retirement should remain a staple, high water mark of life! It should not only be celebrated and even honored for its historical significance but also allowed to continue to evolve and take on fresh ideas and shapes. This all may not happen overnight, but rest-assured, positive change will take shape.

About The Author

Robert Laura is the founder of the Retirement Coaches Association and RetirementProject.org. He is the leading voice for the retirement coaching industry and has pioneered many tools and resources to help people prepare for the non-financial aspects of retirement including the Certified Professional Retirement Coach (CRPC) training and designation. He is the author of several books and guides including *Naked Retirement* and *Retirement Rx*. He is also a nationally syndicated columnist for *Forbes.com* and *Financial Advisor Magazine*. Robert is a sought-after corporate trainer, speaker, consultant, and financial expert witness. He can be reached at rl@robertlaura.com.

About The Retirement Coaches Association

The Retirement Coaches Association is a group of dedicated professionals who are committed to helping people thrive in this next phase of life! Our goal is to not only help you see and experience retirement in a truly different and more meaningful light but also to help you:

- Formulate your vision for your future.
- Unlock and expand your potential.
- Reinforce and maximize your strengths.
- Formulate a plan to keep you relevant, connected, and active.
- Provide encouragement and objective feedback.
- Develop balance in your life now and in the future.
- Support your efforts and provide you with increased confidence.
- Brainstorm strategies to accomplish your goals.
- Uncover and assist in developing your unique abilities.
- Inspire you toward continuous improvement and unparalleled results.

To find a coach near you or to learn more about the organization and our mission to change the focus of retirement planning, please visit RetirementCoachesAssociation.org.

Made in the USA
Columbia, SC
05 March 2021